W9-APK-096

Letterwork

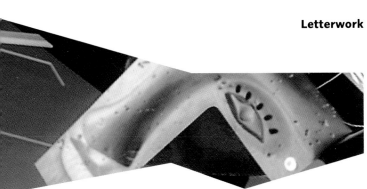

Letterwork

Creative Letterforms in Graphic Design

Brody Neuenschwander

Phaidon Press Limited
Regent's Wharf
All Saints Street
London N1 9PA

Phaidon Press Inc.
180 Varick Street
New York, NY 10014

www.phaidon.com

First published 1993
Reprinted in paperback 1993, 1994, 1997, 1998, 2001, 2004
© 1993 Phaidon Press Limited

ISBN 0 7148 2909 9

A CIP catalogue record for this book is available from the
British Library.

Printed in China

Typeset in Foundry Old Style and Foundry Sans.

Photographic acknowledgement: pictures page 114, page 149
(from *Fuse 1*, 'Intervention') and page 120 (from *Fuse 2*, 'Runes')
©Fontshop International

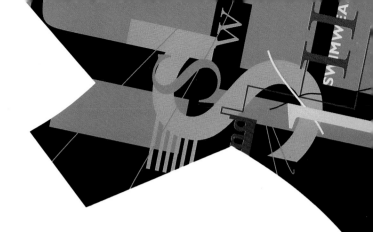

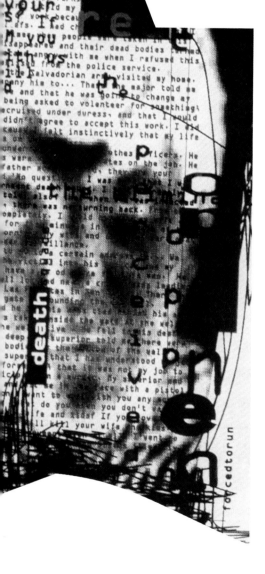

Contents

Introduction

Experimental Lettering
An image composed of dry
transfer lettering and found
typography was
transformed on a Canon
colour copier over many
generations to create the
image seen on the
preceding page. The image
was moved on the glass
between each colour scan,
thus separating the yellow,
cyan and magenta colour
printings. This process was
repreated several times with
the addition of new artwork
at later stages.

LETTERING AND DESIGN
Leonard Currie, London

Introduction

Many graphic designers refer to all letters, including written, drawn and computer-generated letters, as 'typography'. This term tends to suggest that letters come from catalogues and only need be inserted into artwork before printing. But many designs require specially made letterforms to achieve the right effect.

This book is about the making of letters for specific purposes. Compiling it has been like conducting a market survey on the graphic design profession. Designers from around the world were asked to send examples of 'hand-lettering' for possible inclusion. But before requests for transparencies of hand-lettering could be sent out, the term itself had to be defined. Clearly calligraphy, drawn letterforms and letters produced by other hand techniques were well within the scope of the book. But modern graphic design also relies heavily on manipulated type and on letterforms designed on the computer. These could not be left out. The term hand-lettering has therefore been used here in the widest possible sense: virtually any kind of letter specially designed for graphics - with the most rigorous exception of type used straight from catalogues or software - is included. The theme uniting all the letters found here is that they were made for specific purposes and applied to particular designs.

The book has two aims. The first is to show the remarkably high standard being set by the best lettering artists and designers in the world today. From the classical and elegant calligraphic forms of Julian Waters to the sculptural purity of the work of Takenobu Igarashi to the dynamic television sequences of Morgan Sendall, letterforms of the highest quality are being produced for graphic design. The strength and variety of the work illustrated here will provide inspiration for those with a passion for letters and for those who may not yet realize fully what letters can do. The second aim of this book is to help create a new partnership between graphic designers and lettering artists. In the past, art directors and graphic designers have not been entirely aware of the many talented lettering artists working around the world. This book not only provides an analysis of the most important lettering styles and techniques, it gives a world directory of lettering artists and a simple method for commissioning hand-lettering when it cannot be produced in the graphic design studio. Problems of style, emotional impact and

Television Title Sequence
The title sequence for *Horizon*, which received the Bronze Medal at the British Design Awards in 1991, was designed to introduce the world's longest-running science documentary series. Specially commissioned models were developed from storyboards and carefully arranged over two days for a shoot using 35mm film on a motion control rig. The sequence depicts a journey through science-related objects which finally resolve themselves into the word 'Horizon'. Though a Quantel Harry was used in post-production to integrate a series of shoots, the designer was at pains to avoid the dominance of a computer graphics style in the final version. The result is an example of letterforms which contain a narrative meaning and are full of visual excitement.

DESIGN Liz Friedman, London
MODEL MAKING Alan Kemp, London
CAMERA AND LIGHTING Doug Foster
HARRY OPERATION Rob Harvey
Produced at the BBC Television Studios, London

composition are analysed. Using the simple guidelines given here, the designer can identify the right style of tailor-made lettering for a particular job and describe his or her requirements to the lettering artist.

The forms presented here range from spontaneous calligraphic marks to highly refined letters produced on the personal computer. They may have originated with the designer or have been received as type and manipulated in some way. Not all manipulations are dramatic. Included here is the full range: both logos involving very subtle adjustments to type and compositions in which typographic forms have been cut, squeezed, filled with texture and colour and integrated into complex multimedia images. The letters may be legible or illegible, the principle elements in a design or partners for photographs or illustrations. They appear on record sleeves, posters and packaging, in film and television sequences and in a variety of three-dimensional applications. Their effects can vary from the sophisticated to the nostalgic, from the warm and intimate to the crude and violent. And they communicate on other levels as well, using symbols, references, humour, irony, illustrations and codes. Hand-lettering is a fully developed medium of expression with an essential role in graphic design today.

The premise of this book is that specially made letterforms can do things that type cannot do without manipulation. Hand-lettering can provide a sense of movement that is alien to type. It can be tailor-made to fill spaces in layouts that type could never satisfactorily occupy. Letters can be designed and made to suit the style of a particular image, whether photograph or illustration; and they can be carefully conceived to contrast in style, weight and texture with any typeface. Where legibility is not an important consideration, letterforms can create dramatic compositions of shapes and spaces with far more visual interest than the highly legible forms of type. Moreover, hand-lettering powerfully conveys emotions, associations and subliminal information that the restrained forms of type can communicate only in a limited way.

Recent technological developments have made the use of hand-lettering in designs for print a very simple matter. The personal computer allows any hand-made image to be scanned and included in

Exhibition Poster
Koichi Sato is one of the leading proponents of hand-lettering in the world of Japanese graphic design. This poster undertaken for the National Museum of Modern Art, Tokyo in 1990 achieves a powerful and yet sophisticated impact by placing Koichi Sato's own elegant brush-made calligraphy within a geometrically precise composition. The words 'Graphic design today' appear at the top in Latin characters written in the style of the Japanese grass script. The same letters are then scattered over the slopes of Mount Fuji below, symbolizing the meeting of East and West in the world of contemporary graphic design. The contrast between the freely written letterforms and the geometric background is softened by means of textures and airbrushed 'haloes'.

LETTERING AND DESIGN
Koichi Sato, Tokyo
CLIENT National Museum of Modern Art, Tokyo

Poster
for the 1988 Olympics
Unlike Ott + Stein's 'Berlin,
Berlin' poster, which
depends entirely on the
forms of the letters, Ahn
Chung-Un's design
advertising the 1988
Olympics in Seoul uses
lettering as a secondary
decorative feature to
provide a softly coloured
border around the
photographic image of
whirling dancers in
traditional Korean dress.
The Korean characters are a
modernized version of the
ancient seal script, and
roughnesses in their
outlines suggest a stamped
or sealed quality. Above
and below the dancers, the
characters gradually merge
into the space of the
photograph. A traditional
design with a restrained
high-tech quality, this
poster announces Korea's
entrance into the modern
industrial world with its
ancient traditions intact.

LETTERING AND DESIGN
Ahn Chung-Un, Seoul,
S. Korea
CLIENT International
Olympic Committee

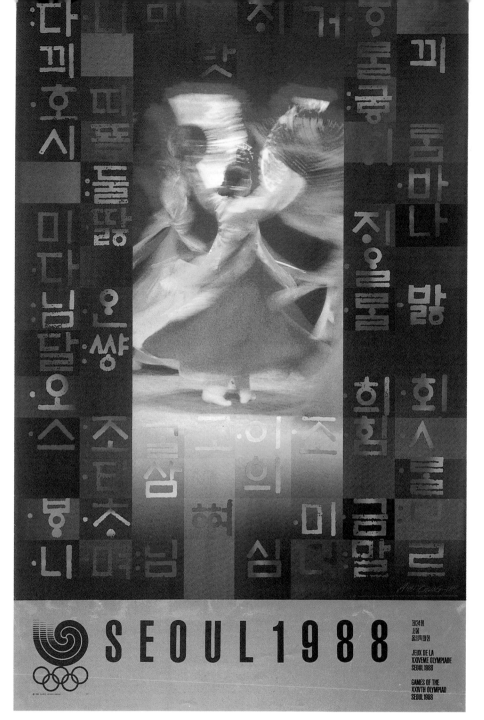

a layout. It is even possible now to go straight from the screen to film and avoid paste-up altogether. The designing of letters on the screen or for scanning will therefore be increasingly important in the next few years.

But while the computer has facilitated the designer's access to hand-lettering, it must not be forgotten that more basic layout techniques can also take full advantage of tailor-made letters. Each stage in the development of print technology in the nineteenth and twentieth centuries (lithography, photo-gravure, photo-lithography, four-colour process) has increased our ability to reproduce the ephemeral qualities of hand-made marks. The only thing that is often missing is the designer's ability to create and manipulate letters. Insufficient educational opportunities are often to blame for this deficiency on the part of many designers. The detailed study of letterforms and the principles of their construction have been increasingly marginalized in the curriculum of many schools of graphic design since the 1960s. Until this time the study of calligraphy, drawn letters, classical inscriptions and other historical material formed an integral part of the training of typographers and designers and gave a firm formal foundation for the design of letters. Experimental studies could then be based on a sound knowledge of underlying form.

These foundations have been eroded over many years, partly because subjects such as calligraphy have been viewed by many typographers as irrelevant to their discipline. A curriculum increasingly crowded with subjects of a technical nature has left less and less time for such apparent luxuries as the careful copying of ancient inscriptions or the study of the formal characteristics of the broad pen. Experimentation has continued, but often without the formal background that could guide it and give it purpose. According to one German teacher of typography, experiments carried out in this void often yielded interesting results at first; but students with no formal training were incapable of taking their tentative work further through informed self-criticism.

While there are now encouraging signs that the need for formal study is again being recognized, one is mindful of the fact that the desktop revolution has placed type-designing software into the hands

Exhibition Poster
Nicolaus Ott and Bernard Stein produced this highly refined design in 1987 using the simplest of techniques. The main words were drawn and tinted and combined with Univers and Futura to produce camera-ready artwork. The composition is classic, with the words 'Berlin, Berlin' placed at optical centre. Both the style of the lettering and the black background refer frankly to Berlin's troubled place in twentieth-century history. The tinted lettering, which can be read either as emerging from darkness or descending into it, points to the fact that the city has for years been at the edge of light and darkness, peace and war.

LETTERING AND DESIGN
Ott + Stein, Berlin
CLIENT Berliner Festspiel GmbH

IRISH LOVE POETRY
Lunchtime readings by Darragh Kelly
Trinity Hall, 12·30pm., From Nov. 1st ~9th

Poster for a Poetry Reading
If Italo Lupi's design for Dada Cucina displays a sophisticated eccentricity, Suzi Godson's simple poster advertising readings of Irish love poetry in Trinity College, Dublin in 1990 evokes the home-spun intimacy of much Irish literature. Godson was attempting to capture the feeling of traditional Celtic type and imagery. Both the rough-cut letterforms and the silkscreen process used to print the poster contribute to a feeling of warmth and intimacy.

LETTERING AND DESIGN
Suzi Godson, London
CLIENT Trinity College, Dublin

of a generation many of whom do not possess this educational background. The prospect of a rising tide of badly designed type threatens from this direction. An ideal course of study for those interested in the design of letters would be a two-track system, assigning equal importance to the formal foundations of the alphabet (both written and typographic) and to free, experimental work using a variety of tools and techniques. This experimentation should follow the compositional principles of the fine arts such as painting and drawing. If pursued together, each of these areas, formal and experimental, would provide a sort of running commentary on the other.

We are entering a period in which increasing attention is being paid to the forms and arrangements of letters. The personal computer has put kerning and leading options at the fingertips of many people who have never recognized the design potential of letterforms. The esoteric freemasonry of the typographer is gradually being eroded, and this should raise standards all around - particularly as certain sectors of the public are beginning to see that graphic designers, like architects, are in some measure responsible for a great deal of ugliness in the world. The place of lettering in graphic design needs reassesssing by every designer, with a corresponding, urgent review of the place of the study of letterforms in the design schools. Is it possible to be a good designer and a bad typographer? Can one be a good typographer without being aware of the principles of letter design and spacing? One of the aims of this book is to demonstrate that an understanding of the principles of letter design is an excellent foundation for all aspects of graphic design.

In the first section of the book, letters are considered for their emotional impact. The forms are grouped broadly into eight themes according to the emotional message they convey. Examples chosen for this section are generally quite legible and play an important role in conveying verbal information; thus they must balance the requirements of legibility with the need to communicate emotions and associations such as excitement, violence, humour, nostalgia, history and elegance. It emerges that particular emotions can be created by a fairly wide range of lettering styles. The character of line, colour, scale and the context of the letters all contribute to this

DADA, la ricetta di cucina preferita dai palati più esigenti, donne o architetti che siano.

Prendi i migliori materiali. Mettili insieme pezzo per pezzo, badando bene alla solidità e al comfort. Applica le tecnologie più avanzate. Scegli colori nuovi e accostamenti nuovi. Passa tutto al vaglio del gusto più raffinato, ricordando che la bellezza di una cucina non è un lusso

ma una necessità. Metti al lavoro un bravo designer, come George Coslin. Non trascurare alcun particolare, per piccolo che sia. Aggiungi accorgimenti nuovi per risolvere vecchi problemi: come i cassetti montati su cuscinetti. Quando è necessario cambia

radicalmente: come Polidade la prima cucina modulare dai alla z. Oppure Hol.ty · Tol.ty. decisamente tutto ciò che na funzionale. Monta il tutto in e servitene in tutta libertà, ferm di tanto in tanto a mangiarte gli occhi.

Catalogue Cover
This fresh, humorous and elegant design of 1978 was, and seems, almost effortless. Italo Lupi has simply spelt out the name of the client with the fresh cherries, beans, celery and radishes likely to be found in any enlightened kitchen. The result reads easily, of course. It might also be seen to refer to the concept of Dadaism in twentieth-century art, which argued that all is nonsense by making surreal and silly compositions of found objects.

LETTERING AND DESIGN
Italo Lupi, Milan
CLIENT Dada Cucina

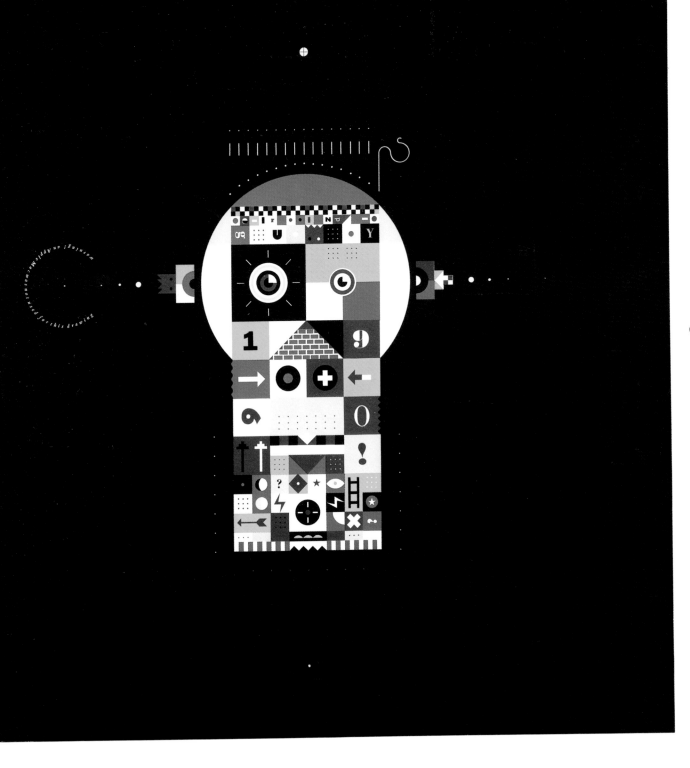

Self-Portrait in Type
The eccentricities of Suzi Godson's poster and Italo Lupi's catalogue cover (pages 16 and 17) are complemented by this 1990 self-portrait in type by the London designer Peter Grundy. The design, produced as a self-promotional print, bears the warning, 'An Apple Mac was not used for this drawing'. Yet its precision, and indeed certain shapes and elements, are drawn directly from the world of Mac design. Grundy's is a wry commentary on the sometimes misplaced zeal for digital design that is currently apparent in the design world.

DESIGN Peter Grundy of Grundy and Northedge

non-verbal impact. The principles of legibility are considered in some detail in order to show how lettering can be manipulated without losing its ability to communicate verbal information.

In section two, letterforms are considered as elements in compositions. Legibility plays less of a role in the work illustrated here, and it is therefore possible to develop shape and line more freely. The problem of choosing the appropriate style of letter is addressed through a range of examples: logos, posters, books and magazines, designs for the music industry, and lettering for film and television. Hand-lettering plays a vital role in all of these areas, from the subtle manipulation of type often required in the design of a logo to the construction of complex mechanized models that are filmed with computer-tracked video cameras.

The interaction of hand-lettering and type is considered in the third part of the book. By analysing the formal and aesthetic characteristics of the major type families, approaches for pairing hand-lettering and type are considered. The manipulation of type is also shown as an aspect of hand-lettering; and the use of calligraphy and the compositional principles of the fine arts in the development of typefaces is addressed.

The next section ties together the different elements of the first three in an effort to identify general principles that can be applied to the design of letters. The structured and legible foundations of typography, which produce even textures and a minimum of formal contrast, are shown to be inadequate for the creation of hand-lettering with strong compositional and emotional impact. This section also contains a detailed catalogue of the techniques used to produce the various letterforms featured in the book, which range from the simple hand techniques available in any studio to unusual and innovative uses of the photocopier and process camera, from special print finishing techniques to computer-generated lettering. It is hoped that these examples may prove useful in a creative crisis.

The brief final section points the way towards the future of lettering. At the end of the book a directory gives the names and studio addresses of the lettering artists and graphic designers whose work is featured here, as well as many others around the world who specialize in the design of letters. This first global listing of lettering

Bicycle Transfers
Despite Peter Grundy's witty renunciation of the Apple Mac in his self-portrait (left), the machine does of course have its uses, the application of hand-lettering and type to three-dimensional objects being one of them. Checkland Kindleysides were able to roll out the shapes of the frames and forks of twelve Saracen mountain bikes using the Mac in order to produce and refine letterforms that would wrap around the forms in the right way. Flat camera-ready artwork for the printing of transfer patterns could be produced in the full knowledge of what the final effect would . be. Designed in 1991.

LETTERING AND DESIGN
Checkland Kindleysides, Rothley, Leicestershire
CLIENT Saracen Bikes

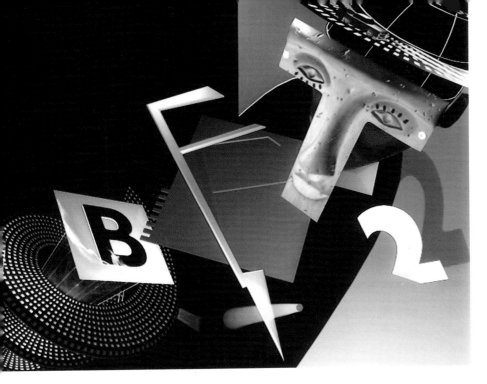

Television Title Sequence

The most sophisticated technology can be brought to bear in the design and production of hand-lettering. The 1990 identity and title sequence for the BBC programme *BFT2* is a case in point. BFT2 is the central character of the programme. The designers wanted to produce a programme identity that integrated the person of BFT2 with the lettering rather than separating the live-action imagery from the type. As the sequence proceeds and BFT2 is confronted by letters emerging from different directions, he strains backwards to pull on a mask in the shape of the letter T, thus resolving both his own identity and the logo or title of the programme. Finally, the number '2' slices into the scheme. The sequence was produced by integrating live-action film and computer graphics on Paintbox.

DESIGN Jane Wyatt and Maylin Lee of the BBC Presentation Design Group, London

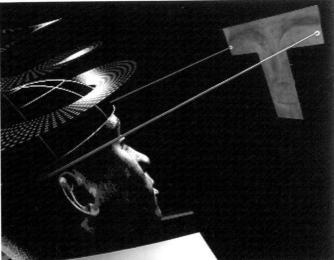

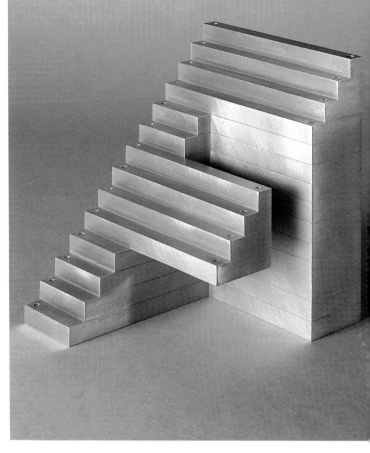

artists is intended for designers and art directors who seek to place special commissions. However, it should be noted that many whose work is shown are not limited to the styles illustrated; nor was it possible to include everyone whose work merits attention. Any additional information will be welcomed by the publishers.

A list of national and regional typography and design societies has also been included, as well as the few societies of calligraphers and lettering artists of a professional kind that exist. The secretaries of these organizations can often help to locate individuals who have specialist skills.

The artists and designers represented in this book work in a variety of professional situations. Many of them are freelance specialists in one form of lettering or another; others are type designers or graphic designers with a special interest in hand-lettering. All share an enthusiasm for letterforms that goes well beyond the financial rewards that good design can bring.

Every effort has been made to gather contributions from the best lettering artists and graphic designers working in the world today. Particularly exciting material is available from Japan, where graphic designers seem able to take a fresh and highly abstract view of the Latin alphabet. The Western world has a great deal to learn from a culture which for over a thousand years has seen its own written forms not only as vehicles for verbal information but also as abstract shapes with powerful emotional qualities. The example of Japan also shows that adequate resources are necessary for real innovation. An artist only asks for the opportunity to do his best.

This book must convince many that recent developments in Western calligraphy and lettering for graphic design show a new sense of the formal potential of the Latin alphabet, and it is hoped that in time the importance of these developments will also be realized by a wider public.

Sculpture
Some of the most astonishing applications of technology to the design and production of letters occur in the work of Takenobu Igarashi, who makes purely sculptural forms on the theme of individual letters. This magnificently crafted sculpture of brushed steel (1990) takes the form of a stack of thick metal plates of various shapes. The three-dimensional form resembles the letter 'A'. But Igarashi is playing here on the relationship between the two-dimensional world of letterforms and the three-dimensional world of sculpture: it is in the step pattern formed by the ascending plates that the intended letter 'F' is revealed.

LETTERING AND DESIGN
Takenobu Igarashi, Tokyo

Conveying the Message

The emotional impact of letterforms

Experimental Lettering
This piece began as a
sculpture of cut and rolled
white paper set up in the
design studio. Green, red
and blue light was cast onto
the sculpture using slide
projectors with coloured
filters. The projector with
the red filter also contained
a 35mm transparency of the
typography. The illuminated
sculpture was then
photographed using a
hand-held camera.

LETTERING AND DESIGN
Leonard Currie, London

Conveying the Message

Letterforms are the most important means of communication available to the graphic designer. They serve the essential function of conveying verbal information; they also carry emotional and aesthetic information that has an impact on how the verbal message is read; and they play a part in the design itself and must relate to the other elements of the composition.

Lettering and typography are therefore central to the design process and cannot be treated as mechanical operations to be considered in relation to the design at the last stage. The question of letterforms must be considered at the beginning; and a lettering style which conveys the appropriate emotional and aesthetic information must be selected (in the case of type) or produced (in the case of lettering) as the design takes shape.

This chapter will celebrate and examine how lettering that conveys essential verbal information in a legible way can, if successful, at the same time be read on other, more intuitive levels.

Legibility

Legibility has been described as a 'certainty of deciphering'. The question is, deciphering of what? Most designers will have argued with a client over the legibility of a proposed approach. The client, who may have in mind the clarity of text type, claims that the design is not instantly legible. The designer may counter that, in the context, it is legible and that it conveys the appropriate non-literal messages as well. The designer and his client are in fact differing over the definition of legibility.

Legibility in its most basic sense does indeed consist of the deciphering of verbal and numerical information without ambiguity. There is a large specialist literature on the physiology, psychology and sociology of reading (see Further Reading for further details). Much of what needs saying on the subject is common sense. All writing systems, to be legible, must observe two laws. First, the letterforms within a system must show sufficient formal contrast to allow efficient recognition of the individual characters. Second, they must show sufficient formal harmony to allow efficient eye travel. In various times and places these two laws have been observed in different ways.

Sculptural Street Address
Letters (and indeed
numbers) carry information
on many levels below the
literal surface. This
magnificent sculpture,
undertaken in 1990, serves
as a street address at the
offices of Nike; the number
'180' has acquired a power
and solidity that inspires
feelings of awe. The forms
have been built up with
layers of brushed-steel
plates, perfectly engineered
and bolted together. The
sculpture bears a striking
similarity to the inside of a
bank vault door.

LETTERING AND DESIGN
Takenobu Igarashi, Tokyo
CLIENT Nike

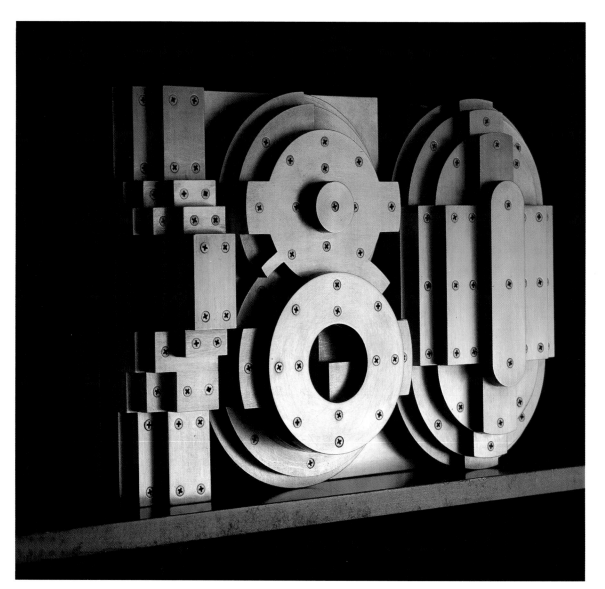

Western alphabets, which include the Latin, Greek, Hebrew and Cyrillic traditions, as well as modern efforts to record aboriginal languages in Africa and the Americas, are phonetic; that is, they record sound values. These systems are based on the fewest possible contrasting shapes, usually geometric in origin, all occupying roughly similar spaces. The characters are few in number and can be learned quickly. Historically, the sheer simplicity and geometric basis of these systems has militated against their development into important calligraphic art forms.

In the Arabic system, the basis of the forms is not geometric but cursive (though scholars often apply geometric analysis after the fact), with greater formal contrast and wider differences in size for the various characters than is the case with Western alphabets. Like Western systems, Arabic is phonetic, has few characters and can be learned relatively easily. The strong contrasts inherent in their shapes, sizes and stroke directions have yielded a vigorous calligraphy with strong compositional possibilities.

The Chinese system and its derivatives are symbolic rather than phonetic, though in Japanese a parallel phonetic system has been added. As in Western alphabets, the characters generally occupy similar spaces, but there are vastly different stroke counts and stroke directions from one character to the next. These characteristics have contributed to the development of important calligraphic traditions. The number of characters in these systems is very high and therefore more difficult to learn; contrasts between them must be identified at a more subtle level than in Western or Arabic writing.

A comparison of these three writing traditions shows that legibility can be achieved in very different ways. The contrast of simple geometric forms that lies at the heart of legibility in Western typography is not present in the Arabic tradition, where contrast of stroke size and direction produce character identity, nor in the Chinese and Japanese traditions, where character identity derives from contrast in stroke density and direction. In any case, as is clear from our ability to read even the most dreadful handwriting, the contrasts and harmonies on which legibility depends are as much a matter of context as of absolute formal properties. Marks are identified in the context of other marks; a whole composition of

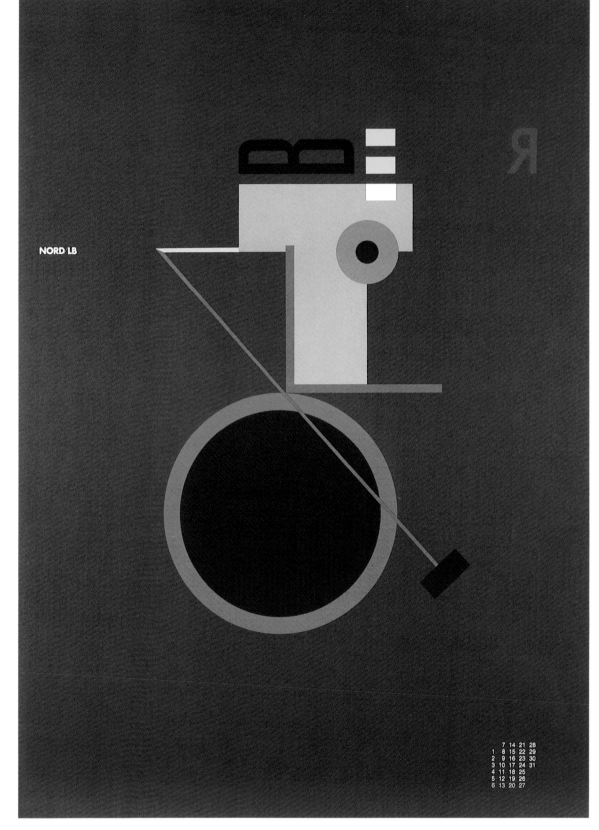

Calendar

Legibility is not always a simple question of deciphering verbal information. Images too can be read, and images built up from letters may be read on several levels. This composition of letters by Ott + Stein, which was produced by photo-composition and traditional paste-up, does not reveal its verbal message until one notices the small block of numbers, bottom right. These are instantly recognizable as the dates on a calendar. As soon as these are identified, the viewer then sees that the composition of letters spells the word 'Oktober'. The clue provided by the numbers allows an intuitive leap in reading the letters.

LETTERING AND DESIGN
Ott + Stein, Berlin
CLIENT Nord Landesbank,
Hannover

marks is itself identified in a context of time, place and culture. All of these factors contribute to the certainty of deciphering. Reading is a culturally based activity, and as such is an aspect – a very important aspect – of the conventions that we all possess and consent to use among ourselves. Legibility is therefore both necessarily tied to the past and renewed and invigorated in the present.

The vocabulary of style

It is said that 'Mere legibility in type is like mere shelter in architecture'. The suggestion is that purely utilitarian typefaces can have little that is visually pleasing about them.

Type is often treated as a completely utilitarian element in graphic design, used only to communicate verbal information in compositions whose strength lies elsewhere, in brilliant photographs, illustrations and abstract shapes. Yet letterforms, even typographic forms, can never be neutral elements in a design. While carrying verbal information, they also invariably convey emotional and associative information as well. We all possess a subtle vocabulary of style that compels us to read a composition involving letterforms on many levels. An elegant copperplate, for example, may signify tradition, quality and a long history of excellence. These values were especially prized by the mercantile and legal culture of the eighteenth and nineteenth centuries, and copperplate was seen to project the right image of respectability and propriety. The connotations can be made clearer still if for instance the swelling lines of copperplate letters are painted in gloss enamel on the side of a vintage delivery van or engraved and printed on expensive paper.

But certain adjustments to these essentially historical forms or to their context will give them very different meanings. Excessively fat copperplate letters that do not keep to the line of writing tend to produce a feeling of whimsy; ragged-edged copperplate manipulated and distressed on the computer may suggest decadence; highly flourished copperplate letters may denote sumptuous extravagance.

These emotional associations are not reserved for historical styles alone. Letters designed to resemble those found on computer printouts, for example, will suggest obvious references to technology, speed and efficiency. But now that digital technology has been with us for a while, certain technical styles may subtly evoke the earlier

Poster
The design by Ott + Stein opposite plays a game of visual hide and seek. In this 1991 poster by John Rushworth and Vince Frost of Pentagram the letter 'A' is turned into an image of the hidden mysteries of the maze. The design was produced on the computer, which makes flawless precision and drop shadows available at the touch of a button. The subject matter is instantly recognizable, allowing the type to be relegated to a marginal role at the top of the poster.

LETTERING AND DESIGN
John Rushworth and Vince Frost of Pentagram, London
ART DIRECTOR John Rushworth
CLIENT *Art and Architecture*

29

Television Title Sequence

The brief for this sequence was to design a generic identity for a long-running series on archaeology in which the different places and periods covered by each programme were evoked. The titling begins by panning across ruins from various eras and countries. At first the viewer assumes the scene to be a real-life setting, then, as the camera pulls out, it becomes clear that each building is actually a letter. Finally, we read 'Chronicle' on a background of sand and rubble.

The title is a 14-foot-long model, shot with a conventional 35mm camera mounted onto a motion/computer-controlled rig suspended from the ceiling with a periscopic lens. Harry was used to blend from one take, lit with heavy shadows, to another take, lit more softly, to add legibility to the logo at the end. The 1988 sequence won the Gold Award at the Imagina competition in Monte Carlo in 1991.

DESIGN AND ART DIRECTION Liz Friedman, London
MODEL MAKING Alan Kemp, London
CEL ANIMATION, LIGHTING AND CAMERA Doug Foster
Produced at the BBC Television Studios, London

years of the computer age, thus carrying with them their own kind of nostalgia. Other high-tech letters may refer to the more negative or sinister aspects of the digital revolution: perhaps surveillance, a mechanized society or the destruction of the natural environment.

Illustrations of styles that have particular associations and emotional connotations in the public mind could be cited almost without end. In lettering we possess a complex grammar by which communication is possible (indeed inevitable) below the literal surface. The designer must therefore develop expertise in this complex process.

The range of associations

The emotional impact of letterforms is communicated before their literal content, and therefore the designer must establish from the outset of a particular project the precise feelings and associations that he or she wishes his design to communicate. In most cases the brief will specify the public that the project is intended to reach. It may also specify the style of lettering required or simply identify the emotions and associations that the lettering and overall design should elicit from the viewer. The job of the designer is then to find the visual language that will be understood in the correct way by the market in question.

Examples of lettering in this chapter are organized into eight broad groupings, each category representing a set of related emotions or associations. Within each, a variety of examples of lettering by some of the world's leading lettering artists and graphic designers communicate these connotations in a clear and powerful way. The reader will observe that the lettering in each broad grouping, though not all of the same style, nevertheless produces generally similar feelings – a point enforced even more by the examination of lettering in other languages. Their emotional impact is communicated without being able to read their verbal content. The wide range of styles represented in each grouping should demonstrate that no one style represents exclusively one emotional state. It should also be evident that the broad groupings given here are by no means all that could be defined, and are, to a degree, inevitably arbitrary and subjective in nature. But it is to be hoped that they will provide a springboard for thought and inspiration.

Video Logo
Unlike the *Chronicle* sequence opposite, the letters for this logo design were constructed on the computer to resemble three-dimensional objects. Light sources shot on film were manipulated on the computer and integrated with the letterforms. The result assumes a high level of sophistication and intelligence in the young audience.

DESIGN Jane Fiedler of the BBC Presentation Design Group, London

Poster
The limits of legibility are astonishingly broad. In this 1989 poster the identity of the four large letters is little more than hinted at. Legibility here depends as much on context as on the hand-drawn letterforms, which are built up of post-modernist fragments. The letters 'T' are 'Y' seem to extend subtly beyond the surface of the poster, while the other letters remain rigorously flat.

LETTERING AND DESIGN
Toshiyasu Nanbu, Osaka
CLIENT Tokyo Designers
Space

June 5[Mon.]–17[Sat.],1989
12:00 A.M. – 7:00 P.M.
TOKYO DESIGNERS SPACE
TYPOGRAPHY WORKS OF TOSHIYASU NANBU

Conveying the Message

Decoding the message

It is a stimulating exercise to decode several of the designs presented in this chapter and to analyse how the designer has given form to the literal and emotional meaning he intends to convey. Pierre Bernard, for example, undertook a project for Parilux, a range of papers recently introduced by ISTD Fine Paper (see page 48). The advertisement design was intended to be seen by consumers of fine-quality paper, in particular discriminating designers, through trade journals for the design industry. The context, then, was that of magazine pages packed with tightly set text, dazzling colour imagery and a jumble of highly designed advertisements, many incorporating special effects and complex images. The audience is supposedly sophisticated, and yet is confronted here with a page nearly blank except for the scrawled, inky, smudged and anything but calligraphic letters of the word 'Parilux'. The size and tilt of the writing are clearly intended to grab the reader's attention: the verbal 'shout' is an age-old technique. But it is the smudges and the childish, unfinished and undesigned quality of the letters that makes one stop and think.

The effect is heightened by the smooth finish of the paper, which suggests for a split second that the marks are freshly made on the page, perhaps still wet. This *trompe l'œil* graffiti or doodle, then, is a visual trick that causes the viewer to realize with extreme clarity that Parilux paper is capable of holding the finest printing details with complete faithfulness. Though not beautiful by the standards of the great calligraphic traditions, it communicates the intended message with force and efficiency.

Another arresting device is employed by Liz Friedman in her identity for BBC television's weekly history programme 'Chronicle'. As the programme opens the viewer's attention is immediately grabbed by dramatic shots of massed architectural ruins, buildings resonant with associations of antiquity, the mysteries of the past and the treasures recovered by archaeology. The camera then begins a slow ascent, finally revealing at a certain level that the ruins are the letters of the word 'Chronicle', products of the modelmaker's art. At this moment the viewer's intellect is assailed by the transformation that has taken place in his own perceptions, a process that reflects perfectly the aims of the programme, which are to deepen the public's interest in history and archaeology and change their expectations of a subject perceived by some as dull.

Exhibition Poster
Illegible calligraphic marks can communicate information as effectively as legibly written forms or type. This 1988 poster by Vaughan Oliver and Chris Bigg displays calligraphy of an undeniably Japanese flavour. The textures and silhouette of the large green shape in particular refer to shoji, Japanese sliding screens. Yet the colours and lines lack the serenity generally associated with traditional Japanese art, positioning the work clearly in the modern era.

LETTERING Chris Bigg, London
DESIGN Vaughan Oliver of V23, London
CLIENT Victoria and Albert Museum, London

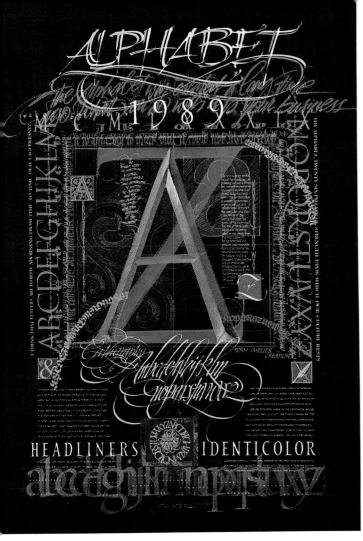

Calendar Cover
John Stevens is equally
skilled with pen, brush and
pencil. This classically
centred composition,
undertaken in 1988, is built
up from an enormous
variety of calligraphic
elements. Most were made
for this design, though
others have been taken
from earlier artwork to
produce a sort of collage.
The resulting cover relies
not on its literal content but
on the beauty of the
letterforms and rich colours
to advertise the product.

LETTERING AND DESIGN
John Stevens, East
Meadow, New York
CLIENT Headliners
Identicolor

Both examples of lettering just quoted contain information well beyond the merely legible. In both cases the non-verbal message is specific, and points to a transformation of the viewer's perceptions. A recent development in graphic design depends on less specific, more intuitive mental leaps to construct a full reading of an image. This development is known in some circles as 'deconstruction', and comes to graphic design from the worlds of the fine arts and literary criticism. Briefly put, literary deconstruction proposes that words have their meaning entirely from their context and not from their references to objects or ideas; the meaning of novels or poems resides in the system of words that make up the text.

The work of Joan Dobkin of the Cranbrook Academy in the United States and of Christopher Priest of Why Not Associates in London both show the influence of deconstruction on the world of graphic design. An analysis of Joan Dobkin's campaign for Amnesty International (see pages 60-61) will illustrate the concept. The campaign poster's distorted type and agitated drawing style, combined with a face that appears ambiguously as either threatened or threatening, is meant to express the anxiety and terror experienced by victims of the repressive political and military system that has existed for many years in El Salvador.

Text and imagery are layered and fragmented in such a way that the reader must piece together both the verbal and the visual clues to understand the message. Key words are emphasized, and where these are not entirely legible, the reader must plunge into a mass of confused lines to decode them. The meaning of the poster is deconstructed by the designer in order that the viewer can reconstruct it in the language of his own experience. Such an approach to design requires a serious commitment to research into the meanings and images associated with the job in question.

In the examples considered above the viewer becomes aware of his own mental actions. He thinks and is aware of receiving information. A good deal of lettering depends on communicating information at the subliminal level. Inasmuch as the viewer is unaware of receiving a message that is specifically encoded in the design, he is being manipulated.

Subliminal advertising and manipulation are a hot topic. It is recognized in the design world, and increasingly by the public, that this can be a real source of abuse in public life. Logos and corporate identites are frequently aimed at the lowest possible level of reception, on the assumption that the public cannot be relied on to make an intelligent response. In other cases the public's impressions are subtly manipulated by exaggerated or false claims, and this process can be supported by the designer. An important theme throughout this book is that a good design communicates to both the intelligence and intuition of the viewer.

The picture on page 42 illustrates a superb piece of lettering involving a subtle kind of manipulation. It shows a design for a t-shirt made for a 'wet and wild' beach party held in Las Vegas in 1990. The design is simple: a block of eccentric brush-made letters coloured randomly with red, yellow, brown and purple. A fresh and childish sun is painted in yellow behind the letters, which are easily legible and impart a sense of childlike play. The innocent style of the poster encourages viewers to set aside any reservations they may have about entertainments of this kind. The message is conveyed only at the subliminal level, however, and is not intended to surface in the viewer's mind.

Such examples confirm that lettering communicates on many levels and that the reading of an image is a complex operation involving intuition and intellect, conscious and subconscious processes. The legibility that the designer of letters seeks to achieve, therefore, is not unimpaired literal legibility, but the complete reading at all levels of the elements of a design. Choosing the appropriate lettering for a particular project can be broken down into reasoned steps that allow creative inspiration to make its entrance. The first step may usefully be to make a clear and brief statement of the emotions and associations that the design is intended to comm-unicate, and to consider from the beginning what style of lettering best serves these ends.

Exhibition Banner
New York Public Library has long been known for its magnificent large-scale banners, which grace its frontage throughout the year. For the lettering artist they pose especially difficult problems of scale: lettering that works on a small-scale mock-up may not retain its grace and elegance when enlarged to a width of 12 to 15 feet. For this design of 1988, John Stevens has chosen an elegant script written with broad pen but related to copperplate, whose style recalls letterforms used for captions in early zoological and botanical treatises.

LETTERING John Stevens, East Meadow, New York
ART DIRECTION Marilyn Lund, New York
CLIENT New York Public Library

Direct Mail Advertisement

In this direct mail advertisement for an apparel manufacturer, Koichi Sato refers to the artistic style of the Momoyama period and especially to the calligraphy and screen paintings of artists such as Hon'ame Koetsu and Ogata Korin. The elegant, watery, hand-drawn calligraphy - which can be seen as reflecting the qualities of the limpid fabrics of Jurgen Lehl's clothing - is almost entirely abstract, and required small typographic notes to be legible. Where Momoyama artists applied discs of leads or silver to paper screens to represent the heavenly bodies, Koichi Sato applies a photograph of the earth, and a 'half-moon' of beige silk. The Mondrian-esque fragment in the upper right-hand corner brings the design back into the Western hemisphere with a gentle bow. Historical sources have been used successfully in 1983 to suggest that the exquisite silks of ancient Japan have their modern counterpart in the clothing of Jurgen Lehl.

LETTERING AND DESIGN
Koichi Sato, Tokyo
CLIENT Jurgen Lehl

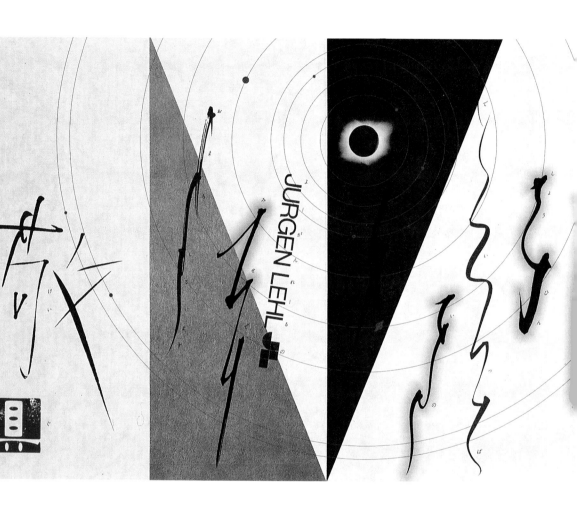

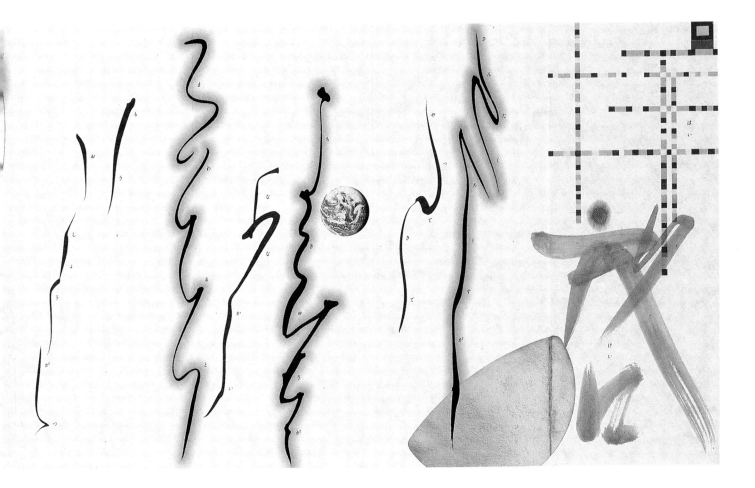

Television Identity

This 1989 television identity sequence by Simon Martin for English Markell Pockett uses a combination of hand-drawn animation, live action film footage and graphics produced using Quantel Paintbox. The lettering was printed on a thin sheet of rubber which was twisted by hand, filmed under a rostrum camera and incorporated with the animation. All these elements were combined using Quantel Harry. The result is a sequence that assumes a high level of visual imagination in the young audience for which it is intended.

LETERING AND DESIGN
Simon Martin for English Markell Pockett, London
PRODUCTION
Jayne Marshall
CLIENT ITV Association

Poster for a Competition

Mitsuo Katsui's design for the 1987 Morisawa type design Awards relies on great economy of form and colour to produce an effect of supreme sophistication. The type was graduated on the photo-typesetter to suggest the emergence of the letters from the background. The vapour trails of the small coloured letters are always at 45 degrees to the vertical and always the same length, which produces an effect of controlled movement. There is thus a sense of restrained power that is entirely in keeping with the principles of type design.

LETTERING AND DESIGN
Mitsuo Katsui, Tokyo
CLIENT Morisawa

Poster for a Charity Run
Letters need not be classically balanced to achieve an effect of sophistication and elegance. The energetic calligraphy produced by Georgia Deaver in 1988 for this poster advertising a sponsored run pulses with the easy power of a confident runner. The light weight of the letterforms, which were written with a ruling pen, prevents them seeming aggressive or frenetic.

LETTERING Georgia Deaver, San Francisco
DESIGN Bill Cooke, San Francisco
ILLUSTRATION Ron Graver
CLIENT The Beacon House

Calendar Cover
The drawn Roman capitals produced by Julian Waters for the 1991 Audubon nature calendar display a degree of simple elegance that would have been difficult to achieve with type. The letters are light in weight and classical in form, two characteristics rarely found in display faces. The proportions are perfectly balanced, whereas mechanically enlarged text type would show distortions and irregularities on this scale.

LETTERING Julian Waters, Washington DC
DESIGN Janet Tingey
CLIENT MacMillan Publishing Inc

Advertisement for a Sweet
The ability of hand-lettering to convey humour and even silliness is well demonstrated by this ad for Smarties. Two-dimensional letterforms are combined with three- dimensional candies to produce a visual riddle in the form of a clock. Upper- and lower-case letters are expanded, condensed and bent to form the silhouette of the clock's hands. Quieter, more secret letters hint that Only Smarties have the answer'. The use of randomly mixed and brightly coloured upper- and lower-case letters to represent the writing of a child is a commonplace in graphic design. Yet this advertisement, which in 1991 was part of a long-running campaign, achieves a welcome freshness by making light of a very familiar situation.

LETTERING
Kira Josey, London
DESIGN AND ART DIRECTION
Billy Mawhinny of J. Walter Thompson, London
CLIENT
Rowntree Mackintosh

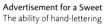

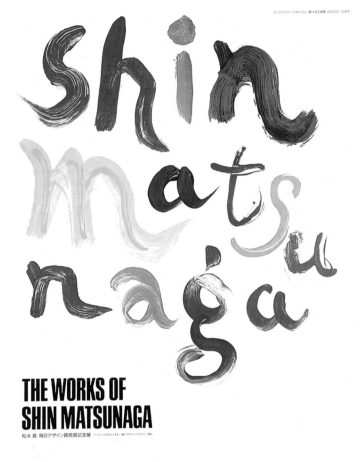

**THE WORKS OF
SHIN MATSUNAGA**

**Exhibition Poster and
Special Event Stationery**
For an exhibition of his
work held at the Ginza
Graphic Gallery in Tokyo in
1989, Shin Matsunaga
produced this special event
logo using a large brush
and bright colours on
coated paper. The childlike
exuberance of the letters
would be difficult for many
adults to achieve, and their
use as a personal and
corporate identity is very
surprising indeed. Yet one
cannot but be impressed by
their joyful enthusiasm, a
quality which one is
inclined to attribute to the
designer himself. This
sense of the personal is part
of all hand-lettering, and
sets it apart from type.

LETTERING AND DESIGN
Shin Matsunaga, London
POSTER CLIENT
Ginza Graphic Gallery
STATIONERY CLIENT Shin
Matsunaga Design Inc

T-shirt Design

Margo Chase's T-shirt design for Playboy' s Wet and Wild Beach Party, held in Las Vegas in 1990, uses kooky and eccentric letterforms to impart a feeling of innocent play which might not be associated by everyone with such an event. Nancy Ogami's brush-made letters are intended subtly to change and upgrade the public's perceptions. At the same time, the irrational distribution of weight and the marks' ragged edges also hint at an underlying decadence.

LETTERING Nancy Ogami, Los Angeles
DESIGN Margo Chase, Los Angeles
ART DIRECTION Steve Rechschapfner, Los Angeles
CLIENT *Playboy*

Lettering for a Billboard Advertisement

Letterforms are not only capable of conveying emotional information: they can communicate tactile information as well. The word 'Koalas', written by Iskra Johnson with a brush on watercolour paper, tells us all we need to know about this warm, fat, furry animal. The Germans have a descriptive word for it: 'Fingerspitzengefühl': loosely translated, what our fingertips tell us.

LETTERING Iskra Johnson, Seattle, Washington DC
ART DIRECTION DDB Needham, New York
CLIENT Anheuser Busch

British Painting '74 Hayward Gallery
Arts Council of Great Britain 26 September to 17 November 1974
Monday to Friday 10 to 8/Saturdays 10 to 6/Sundays 12 to 6
Admission 30p/Children, students and pensioners 15p
10p all day Monday and between 6 to 8 Tuesdays to Fridays

Exhibition Poster

Simple, child-like letterforms may serve to communicate a sophisticated message. These letters executed by Alan Fletcher in 1974 refer directly to the work of David Hockney, who introduced a new naiveté into British art following the hyper-conceptual '60s. The crude and playful quality of these letterforms appears as deliberate primitivism: their spontaneity is calculated, and irony has replaced the innocent joy associated with childhood.

LETTERING AND DESIGN
Alan Fletcher of Pentagram, London
CLIENT The Arts Council of Great Britain

Cover for an Illustration Annual

Hand-drawn and painted illustrations are to photography what hand-lettering is to type: the immediacy, energy and graphic qualities of illustration are a vitally important alternative to the three-dimensional illusion of the photograph. In his cover for the 1983 *Illustration in Japan* annual, Shin Matsunaga has captured these qualities by using roughly drawn capitals disposed over equally rough horizontal bands of colour. The piece is suggestive of Western wood-block prints, which are indeed forerunners of modern book illustrations.

DESIGN AND ART DIRECTION
Shin Matsunaga
CLIENT Kodansha Ltd

Exhibition Poster

The artistic sophistication and zest for life that one associates with Barcelona are well caught by this poster announcing an exhibition of Catalan design held in Hamburg in 1989. Ott + Stein have made the name of the show, the Spanish word 'Diseño', the sole element in their composition. The letters are composed of a series of vertical red bars, evenly spaced and all the same height except for the 'i'. These bars are modified, one by one, by simple geometric shapes. The 's' and the 'o' were set in Amati and slipped into the design. By printing this bold composition in the hot colours of the Spanish flag, the effect of a contemporary heraldic banner is achieved - an impression uncompromised by the two small incidental images of designed objects placed below the 'D' of 'Diseño'.

LETTERING AND DESIGN
Nicolaus Ott + Bernard Stein, Berlin
CLIENT Internationales Design Zentrum, Berlin

44

Book Cover
The cover of this 1985 publication on the cosmetics designer Shiseido displays an intense yet detached sensuality. The colours are cool but vibrant, the composition dynamic, yet held in tense balance. Koichi Sato has used abstract calligraphic marks to suggest both letterforms and the features of the female face. The 'halo' around the letters was created with the airbrush. Droplets of paint can be read as beauty marks. The realistically rendered lips, painted in deathly green, create an ambiguous spatial relationship. The viewer can almost hear the stiletto heels clicking on the pavement.

LETTERING AND ART DIRECTION Koichi Sato, Tokyo
DESIGN Kuni Kizawa
CLIENT Shiseido Co, Ltd

Television Title Sequence
In the title sequence of this BBC special programme in 1991 on the Basque separatist movement, Christine Büttner designed and commissioned a 'matador's cape' in raw silk with appliqué lettering encrusted with black glass beads, which was made with extreme care and precision. The cape was flashed before the camera with a matador's flair as the scene of the title sequence changed. As in the design by Ott + Stein opposite, Büttner uses the colours of the Spanish flag. Her letterforms, originally written with a pen, were cut from bright yellow silk, and are bold, restless and aggressive.

LETTERING AND DESIGN Christine Büttner of the BBC Presentation Design Group, London
PROP MAKERS Kier Lusby, London
CLIENT BBC Television

Cover for an Employee Benefits Brochure
The focal point of Julian Waters' composition of 1990 is the word 'Benefits', written in chunky calligraphy, with the tail of the 'f' cutting across the blue space of the cover. Much of the impact of these letters derives from the way in which thin strokes slice through thick ones. Basically italic in form, they were written directly with the broad pen with confidence and skill, and retouched.

LETTERING AND DESIGN
Julian Waters,
Washington DC
ART DIRECTION Jessica
Wilson, Washington DC
CLIENT
The Washington Post

Lettering for Delivery Van
Mosimann's is a top-drawer dining club in central London founded by the renowned chef Anton Mosimann. In designing the logo for this elegant establishment, Ian Logan and Alan Colville turned to the glorious cuisine for inspiration. The artful arrangement of rare foods, enamelled with exquisite sauces, suggested the use of thick brush marks, which have been painted in glowing colours on the sides of the club's Asquith delivery van. Inside the club, the same shapes are stencilled in powdered chocolate on to every cup of frothy cappuccino.

LETTERING Alan Colville of Ian Logan Design Co, London
DESIGN AND ART DIRECTION Ian Logan, London
CLIENT Mosimann's

Poster
for a Cultural Evening
Claude Dieterich's elegant tangle of calligraphic flourishes for this poster of 1985 suggests the excitement of an evening of Latin American music and dance. The feeling of speed, the tactile sensation of pen and ink are communicated to the viewer. Calligraphy, with pen or brush, is especially able to convey excitement.

LETTERING AND DESIGN Claude Dieterich
CLIENT: United States Embassy, Lima

Magazine Advertisement
Pierre Bernard's ad for Parilux papers shows that crude letterforms and the almost shocking impact they can have on the viewer may successfully convey quite a sophisticated message. The smudged letters of the word Parilux, reproduced with forceful clarity on the generally pristine pages of design magazines in 1991, grabbed the readers' attention and at the same time demonstrated the fine reproduction possible on this new art paper.

LETTERING AND DESIGN
Pierre Bernard of the Atelier de Création Graphique, Montreuil
CLIENT I.S.T.D. Fine Paper Ltd

PARIS
IRAK
CHINA
LUZERN
SPAIN
ČSSR

Stencilled Letters from Packing Crates
The way in which letters are made strongly influences their form and emotional impact. Letters stencilled onto packing crates at their place of origin have a crude and spontaneous quality that derives from the immediacy of their production and the simple shapes allowed by the process. Stencilling does not facilitate sharpness and even spacing; the stencils for some letters wear out or are lost, requiring improvization - note the word 'Spain'; and the uneven surfaces of corrugated cardboard and rough-sawn planks cause bleeding and distortion. Yet it is interesting to note that each of the place-names shown here seems to contain something of the character of the place itself.

COLLECTED BY
Hans-Rudolf Lutz, Zürich

Limited Edition Print
The idea of stencilling has
been used by Shin
Matsunaga to produce this
fine print of 1983 on the
theme of industrial exports.
Hand-made letterforms
were scanned into the
computer and manipulated
to produce layering and
texturing. At the centre of
the composition are
fragments of customs forms
and export licences, which
were also scanned in. Shin
Matsunaga has preserved
the crude vigour of crate
stencilling in the forms and
textures of this piece, but
has transformed it into a
work of considerable
beauty and serenity
through colouring, and
through creating a
composition of classical
balance.

LETTERING AND DESIGN
Shin Matsunaga, Tokyo

Television Sequence
All the terror of the Stalinist era is evoked in this sequence designed by Morgan Sendall (1991). The sequence combines live action footage, models and, in scenes not represented here, animation. Post-production was done on Quantel Harry. As the sequence progresses the awesome cyrillic letters of the world 'Stalin' are forged in red-hot steel. Showers of sparks and smoke partially obscure the letters as the hammer strikes home with a terrible ring. Stalin's brutal destruction of all who opposed him is clearly evoked in this remarkable sequence.

LETTERING AND DESIGN
Morgan Sendall, London
CLIENT Philip Whitehead for Thames Television and Home Box Office

WOHLAN / MEIN FREUND /
WIE STEHT ES MIT DER DIKTATUR? IST ES NICHT SO / DASS
SICH DIE DEMOKRATIE SELBER AUFLÖST DURCH EINE
GEWISSE UNERSÄTTLICHKEIT IN DER FREIHEIT?
WENN SICH DIE VÄTER DARAN GEWÖHNEN / IHRE KINDER
EINFACH GEWÄHREN UND LAUFEN ZU LASSEN / WIE SIE
WOLLEN / UND SICH VOR IHREN ERWACHSENEN KINDERN
GERADEZU FÜRCHTEN / EIN WORT ZU REDEN / ODER WENN
DIE SÖHNE SCHON SO SEIN WOLLEN / WIE DIE VÄTER /
ALSO IHRE ELTERN WEDER SCHEUEN / NOCH SICH UM IHRE
WORTE KÜMMERN / SICH NICHTS MEHR SAGEN LASSEN
WOLLEN / UM JA RECHT ERWACHSEN UND SELBSTÄNDIG
ZU ERSCHEINEN.
UND AUCH DIE LEHRER ZITTERN BEI SOLCHEN VERHÄLTNISSEN
VOR IHREN SCHÜLERN UND SCHMEICHELN IHNEN LIEBER /
STATT SIE SICHER UND MIT STARKER HAND AUF EINEN
GERADEN WEG ZU FÜHREN / SO DASS DIE SCHÜLER SICH
NICHTS MEHR AUS IHREN LEHRERN MACHEN.
ÜBERHAUPT SIND WIR SCHON SO WEIT / DASS SICH DIE
JÜNGEREN DEN ÄLTEREN GLEICHSTELLEN / JA GEGEN SIE
AUFTRETEN IN WORT UND TAT / DIE ALTEN ABER SETZEN
SICH UNTER DIE JUNGEN UND SUCHEN SICH IHNEN
GEFÄLLIG ZU MACHEN / INDEM SIE IHRE ALBERNHEITEN
UND UNGEHÖRIGKEITEN ÜBERSEHEN ODER GAR
DARAN TEILNEHMEN / DAMIT SIE JA NICHT DEN ANSCHEIN
ERWECKEN / ALS SEIEN SIE SPIELVERDERBER ODER GAR
AUF AUTORITÄT VERSESSEN.
AUF DIESE WEISE WERDEN DIE SEELE UND DIE WIDER-
STANDSKRAFT ALLER JUNGEN ALLMÄHLICH MÜRBE.
SIE WERDEN AUFSÄSSIG UND KÖNNEN ES SCHLIESSLICH
NICHT MEHR ERTRAGEN / WENN MAN NUR EIN KLEIN
WENIG UNTERORDNUNG VON IHNEN VERLANGT.
AM ENDE VERACHTEN SIE DANN AUCH DIE GESETZE / WEIL
SIE NIEMAND UND NICHTS MEHR ALS HERR ÜBER SICH
ANERKENNEN WOLLEN / UND DAS IST DER SCHÖNE /
JUGENDFROHE ANFANG DER TYRANNEI!   PLATO

JAHRESGRUSS 1992   WERNER SCHNEIDER.

New Year's Greeting

The exquisite letters of this piece of 1985 by Werner Schneider show a profound understanding of early Greek and Roman inscriptional forms chosen in order to give a monumental presence to Plato's words. The letters, which are monoline, were drawn with a pointed pen. They display simple geometric structures, but these are freely written to produce lively forms. The result is a solid block of text that combines an overall sense of stability and calm with warmth and a gentle playfulness. Schneider considers calligraphy and history to be the bedrock of the discipline of type design.

LETTERING AND DESIGN
Werner Schneider,
Wiesbaden
CLIENT Fachhochschule,
Wiesbaden

Cover for a Type Catalogue

The importance of the study of historical and modern calligraphy for the design of type is emphasized by this design for the type catalogue of a Norwegian printing firm, produced in 1990. All the letters were made with a broad pen, with serifs and entasis achieved through manipulation of pen angle and pressure.

LETTERING AND DESIGN
Christopher Haanes, Oslo
CLIENT Allkopi

Limited Edition Screen Print

In this print, undertaken in 1988, Jill Yelland summarizes the role of history in the design of letters. The image was produced to honour and thank Yelland's teacher of typography, Wolfgang Weingart. It was printed using opaque and transparent inks and glazes in five colours, plus special printings with silica and enamel inks. At the centre is the diagramatic 'D' from Albrecht Dürer's book, *Of the Just Shaping of Letters*. The Phoenecian character 'daleth', which gave rise to our letter 'd', emerges as a shadow from the background.

LETTERING AND DESIGN
Jill Yelland, South Perth, Australia

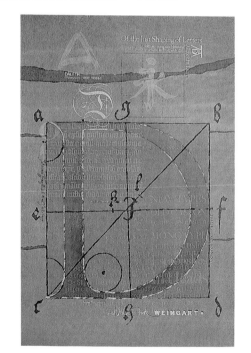

Exterior Signage
Historical letters may be used to create a feeling of nostalgia. The exuberance of the California Gold Rush era spawned a style of lettering that has never lost its vitality in American culture. Derived ultimately from Victorian display faces, these ornamental letters frequently appeared on saloons, casinos and music halls. Their function is little changed today, as this lively sign by Mark Oatis attests. New technology, however, has made even more extravagant effects possible. This sign was constructed of 1/8 inch aluminium panels painted with auto-motive enamels and 23 carat gold. The inscribed letters and ornaments were carved. This sign won first place in the 1992 Commercial Sign Design Competition in the United States.

LETTERING AND DESIGN
Mark Oatis of Smith, Nelson and Oatis Sign Co, Denver
CLIENT Phenix House Casino

Logo
Tony Forster has entered into the spirit of Ragtime with this logo in the style of the Roaring Twenties. These ornamental letters twist and turn to fill the circle with clarinet trills and trumpet blasts. The artwork was produced by hand by one of the masters of expressive lettering.

LETTERING AND DESIGN
Tony Forster
CLIENT Alexander's Ragtime Band

Blackletter

Blackletter, Fraktur and Gothic script are terms of convenience used to describe, in each case, a wide variety of lettering styles. Julian Waters' calligraphy for Ralston Purina and John Stevens' design of the word 'Mozart' might both be described as Gothic and have much in common. Yet subtle differences influence the mood of each. 'Mozart' is more restrained, elegant and courtly: the 'o' has the classic hexagonal blackletter form. Julian Waters gives the 'o's of 'Ralstonius' and so on a more batarde look by curving the left stroke of the letter (compare these to the letter 'e' in 'The Elizabethan Theatre'). The capricious flourishing of the words 'Ralstonius Purinas Copyae Collegium' reminds one of the banners of the small-town American newspaper. Careful attention to seemingly minor points of letter design may produce significant changes in emotional and associative content, as shown by these four 'Gothic' examples.

LETTERING 1,3 and 4 Julian Waters, Washington DC
2 John Stevens, East Meadow, New York

Domäne Geisenheim am Rhein

Het spel van liefde en toeval

Copperplate

Copperplate, like Blackletter, is a broad stylistic category. While it is rare indeed for copperplate letters to leave all historical associations behind, within this category many feelings may be evoked. Werner Schneider's elegant and historically correct wine label speaks of care and connoisseurship. Elmo van Slingerland's letters for a playbill recall the literature of the seventeenth and eighteenth centuries and the soft intimacies of love. The ordered extravagance of the Baroque is clearly expressed by Axel Bertram in his transcription of a passage from Goethe. Finally, David Quay depicts worldly pleasures with the eccentrically flourished words 'Fine Jewellery'. Each has addressed questions of weight, movement and form in a different way.

LETTERING 1 Werner Schneider, Wiesbaden
2 Elmo van Slingerland, Rotterdam
3 Axel Bertram, Berlin
4 David Quay, London

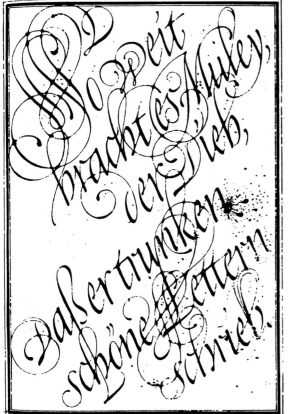

Album Cover

Many of the most extraordinary and surreal images come from the music industry. Vaughan Oliver and Chris Bigg have emerged as leading proponents of counter-culture design. Their cover for Heidi Berry's 1991 album Love displays classic surrealistic symptoms: dream-like images that can only be connected by free association; mad writing; intense and jewel-like colours floating in a sea of leaden grey. Bigg's manic calligraphy serves as a caption to Westenberg's beautifully bizarre photographs. But the lettering is completely illegible and no sense can be made of the images; the word 'love' barely manages to hold its place in a nonsensical world.

LETTERING Chris Bigg, London
DESIGN Chris Bigg and Vaughan Oliver at V23, London
PHOTOGRAPHY Kevin Westenberg
CLIENT 4AD Records

heidi
BERRY

Album : CAD 1012 Cassette : CAD C 1012 Compact Disc : CAD 1012 CD

LOVE

Single Cover
In this design of 1989 by Paul White, Ruth Rowland's funky letterforms suggest an underlying rebelliousness as they rise from the head of Monie Love. Silhouettes reminiscent of African tribal art move among the letters, but this is the world of Western urban blacks, and so these letters also recall graffiti. The distribution of weight is irrational, the forms ungainly. Yet the contending lines balance each other out to produce a stable rectangle. Black subculture is represented as a well-established phenomenon.

LETTERING Ruth Rowland, London
DESIGN Paul White of Me Company, London
CLIENT Chrysalis Records

Logo
In this 1990 logo Margo Chase has captured perfectly the Baroque decadence of the singer Prince. The letterforms, drawn with pen and ink, remind one of the curly wire chairs of Parisian cafés and the painted eyes of '50s *femmes fatales*. There is acute nostalgia here, masked by a strange irony.

LETTERING Margo Chase, Los Angeles
ART DIRECTION Jeri Heiden, Los Angeles
CLIENT Warner Brothers Records

57

Poster
for a Cultural Festival

Art Chantry's monumental poster for the Bumbershoot Festival held in Seattle in 1989 uses the brilliant colour afforded by screen printing to produce the effect of layered graffiti. A rather sinister figure juggles with the letters of the word 'Bumbershoot' and the numbers '1989' while balancing on a bongo board. The board's roller repeats the poster's title in an incongruous Olympic style. Art Chantry explains that the techniques used to create the artwork for this poster were straightforward, even a bit slapdash. The hand-lettering is as rough and energetic as the image. Yet the direct and unrefined approach has yielded an attention-drawing design with vigour and flair.

LETTERING AND DESIGN Art Chantry, Seattle
CLIENT Seattle Arts Commission and One Reel

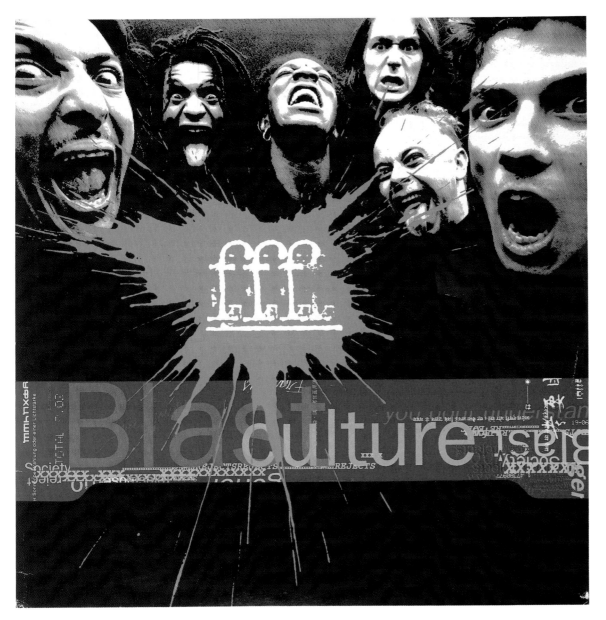

Album Cover
Virtually all of the lettering in this 1991 design is type, much of it taken from packages, maps, labels and other sources. The album title, *fff*, in drastically enlarged typewriter letters, screams at the viewer from a splatter of orange paint. The 'pirated' letterforms were screen-printed to produce artwork then scanned for photo-lithography. Stylorouge use an impressive array of simple studio techniques to achieve striking effects with typographic letters (see the Design of Letters section), especially suited to ephemeral objects.

LETTERING AND DESIGN
Chris Thomson for
Stylorouge, London
ART DIRECTION
Rob O'Connor for
Stylorouge, London
PHOTOGRAPHY
Stephane Sedanoui
CLIENT Epic Records

Promotional Poster and Information Leaflets
Joan Dobkin designed artwork for this poster and informational leaflets and presented it to Amnesty International in 1991 as a potential promotional campaign. The poster weaves together two stories that reveal the appalling political situation in El Salvador. The stories, however, are presented not as narratives but as clues enmeshed in a web of confused lines, forms and colours; the viewer must reconstruct the fragmented message according to his or her own experience. The poster thus works to reform the beliefs of the viewer and to motivate him or her to action.

LETTERING AND DESIGN
Joan Dobkin, Bloomfield Hills, Michigan
CLIENT Amnesty International

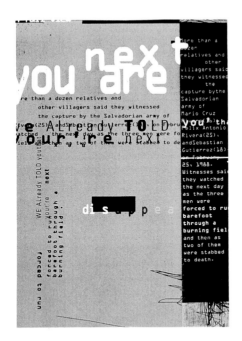

Informational Leaflets for
the Amnesty Campaign
The purpose of the series is
to stimulate interest in the
organization and to
increase its membership; it
exemplifies the principles
of deconstruction in
graphic design. Joan
Dobkin produced these
designs as part of her own
contribution to the work
of Amnesty International.
The series is discussed in
further detail on page 35.

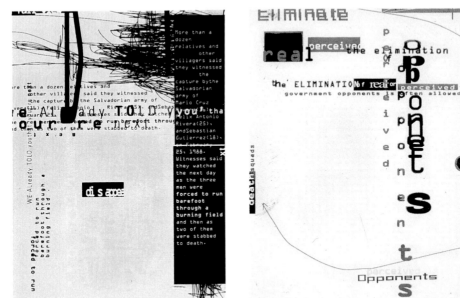

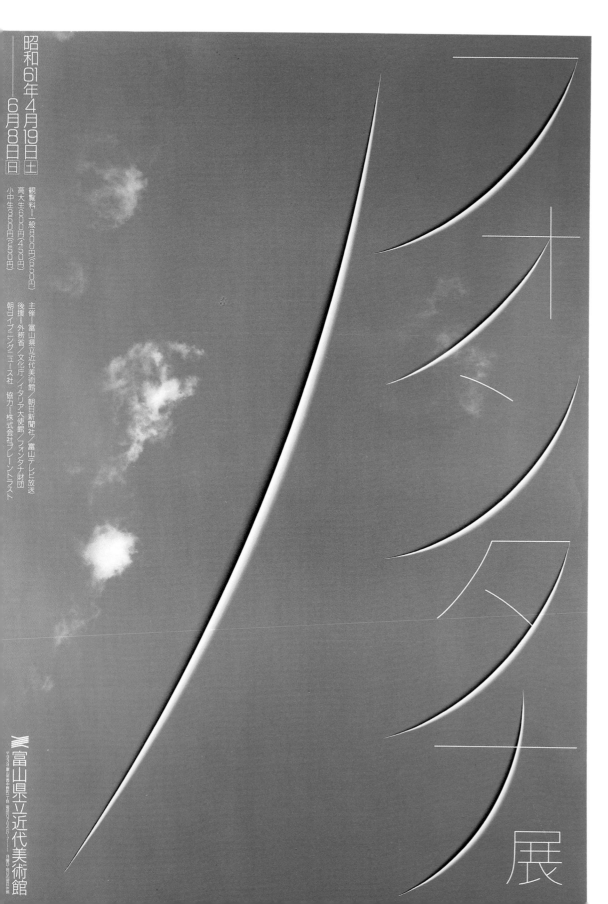

昭和61年4月19日（土）
6月8日（日）

観覧料—一般800円(650円)
高大生600円(450円)
小中生350円(250円)

主催／富山県立近代美術館／朝日新聞社／富山テレビ放送
後援／外務省／文化庁／イタリア大使館／フォンタナ財団
朝日イブニングニュース社　協力—株式会社ブレーントラスト

富山県立近代美術館

フォンタナ展

Exhibition Poster
With this poster of 1986
Kazumasa Nagai perfectly
captured the essence of the
paintings of the American
artist Fontana, who crossed
the boundaries between
abstract expressionism and
conceptual art by slashing
through his canvases with
a knife. Violating the
tradition of the canvas as
window on to an
illusionistic space, Fontana
made real openings in the
picture plane. Yet at the
same time his slashes can
be seen as elegant
calligraphic marks, integral
to the structure of the
painting. Kazumasa Nagai
has used the computer in a
similar way, to produce
illusionistic slashes in a
bright blue sky. The 'cuts'
also form the letters of
the artist's name,
transcribed in the heavens,
as a celebration of the
historical importance of
Fontana's iconoclastic
methods.

LETTERING AND DESIGN
Kazumasa Nagai, Tokyo
CLIENT The Museum of
Modern Art, Toyama

Theatre Poster

Jacques Koeweiden used an impressive economy of form and line in this theatre poster, produced in 1990. A few simple shapes containing images taken from history have been built up into a dynamically balanced composition. The red rectangle containing the author's portrait serves as a clear focal point. The word 'Pirandello', set in Century ITC Bold Extended, is conceived as another essential element. The poster was screen-printed with uv lacquer to provide rich colours and a high-gloss finish.

LETTERING AND DESIGN
Koeweiden/Postma,
Rotterdam
CLIENT Frascati Theatre.

Exhibition Poster

A cool, high-tech style is typified by Shin Matsunaga's poster. The sheer economy of this design was perhaps only to be expected from Japan. This image, produced for the 1991 exhibition entitled *91 Objects by 91 Designers*, is made up of 91 computer-generated metallic pins standing vertically and casting irrational shadows. The concept does not depend on subtle meaning this is a piece of pure design, appropriate and well crafted, whose form itself demands the viewer's undivided attention.

LETTERING AND DESIGN
Shin Matsunaga, Tokyo
CLIENT Gallery 91, New
York

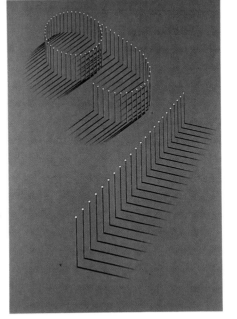

Experimental Lettering

The design potential of the new digital technology is still relatively uncharted territory. In this computer-generated image of 1991, the letters of the word 'VOLOW' were 'loaded' with the tensions of simulated springs, which were then released in order to produce distortions. The computer itself thus played a part in the design process that could not have been foreseen by the designer.

LETTERING AND DESIGN David Small at the Media Arts and Sciences Laboratory, Massachusetts Institute of Technology (MIT)

Billboard (detail)

Modelmaking, lighting, photography and computer technology combine to produce this high-tech display for Smirnoff Vodka in 1990. The letter 'I' from the product name makes reference to Russian constructivism as well as to a style that might be called 'Soviet chic', which rippled through the design world with the ending of the Cold War. Freehand was used to produce a typographic image, which was printed out on 35mm film. This transparency was then used to project the type onto the model. The toy helicopter on its projected launchpad (which repeats the letter to enforce the identity) adds an element of whimsy. It was added during the shoot when the designers noticed the resemblance of the riveted letterforms to skyscrapers.

LETTERING AND DESIGN Why Not Associates, London
MODEL MAKER David Greenwood, London
PHOTOGRAPHER Rocco Redondo
CLIENT Smirnoff/Young and Rubican

Exhibition Poster

Traditional hand and camera techniques can be used to produce dazzling high-tech effects. This poster by Shin Matsunaga was made in 1987 for an exhibition of the work of the Japanese designer Ikko Tanaka. Openings in the shape of the Japanese characters 'Ikko' (one light) were cut in black paper. Coloured films were then placed over the openings and the whole piece was back lit and photographed with a slow exposure time.

LETTERING AND DESIGN Shin Matsunaga, Tokyo
CLIENT Seibu Museum of Art, Chiba, Japan

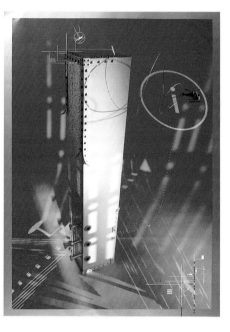

Poster for a Competition
Mitsuo Katsui used the Response program in 1985 to integrate a typographic letter 'O' with a photograph of the patterns made by floating oil in order to produce this image for Morisawa. Harking back to the psychedelic art of the 1960s, it is also a tour de force in the manipulation and integration of distinct images. The 'O' seems to emerge from a creative vortex, thus symbolizing with clarity the aims of this Morisawa type design competition.

LETTERING AND DESIGN
Mitsuo Katsui, Tokyo
PHOTOGRAPHY Karl E. Deckart
CLIENT Morisawa

Lettering as Image

GRID

Experimental Lettering
This complex, layered
image was created on a
Canon colour copier. The
original artwork, made with
dry transfer lettering, was
placed on the glass and
moved after each colour
scan. This separated out the
yellow, cyan and magenta
printings. The process was
repeated ten times using
each new copy as the
artwork for the next
generation. Finally, the
copier's plotting stylus was
used to select rectangular
areas for overprinting in
primary colours. The
spinning effect of the
lettering was achieved by
turning the artwork
between generations.

LETTERING AND DESIGN
Leonard Currie, London

Lettering as Image

In the first section of this book it was established that letterforms communicate their emotional content before their verbal content. It was also shown that there exists a complex grammar that allows us to receive and understand the non-verbal significance of a whole range of lettering styles. In the case of legible letters, the subject of the previous chapter - letters that play an important part in communicating verbal information - their literal and intuitive aspects must be kept in balance. Legible letterforms can make powerful compositions, but there is a limit to the amount of manipulation and distortion the letters can undergo before they become illegible.

The theme of this section is letterforms that are used primarily as elements in a composition. Here legibility is of secondary importance; thus, the letterforms can be designed with greater freedom. Reading gives way here to decoding: letters become abstract shapes or symbols with something more than phonetic content. Letters themselves can be used as images, and these images can be related creatively to the other elements in an overall design. The examples here are selected from a whole range of media, and grouped accordingly into sections on logos, posters, designs for the music industry, books and magazines and lettering for film and television.

The dilemma of style

Every conceivable historical and modern style of lettering is nowadays available to the graphic designer. Indeed style has become a throw-away concept for many designers, used for surface effect and rejected when the next job comes in. This is a uniquely modern phenomenon, and it seems appropriate to look into its origins.

The revival of historical styles and the importation of foreign influences have always occurred to some extent in the history of art. In the nineteenth century all historical styles began to be mined for inspiration by designers, architects and artists alike. For these people, the style was not a matter of mere surface effect: there were fierce battles over the moral, technical and cultural superiority of various historical styles. Impassioned supporters of competing stylistic camps developed detailed and highly esoteric arguments to justify the use of Romanesque, Gothic, Classical and other approaches. In the process the public, presented with bewildering new artefacts in an array of exotic guises, became divorced from the arts. A language of form was being introduced that people could read with only partial success.

Componist
david dramm

edwin kolpa
Toneelbeeld

marc van gelder
Licht

bianca van dillen
Kostuums

Choreografie

1 phil griffin

2 dries van der post en

3 guido severien

dansproduktie

Theatre Poster
This 1990 poster by
Koeweiden/Postma uses
hand-drawn letters as
important elements in the
composition. The word
'tiga', which moves from
the wide margin at the left
of the poster into the
principal blue background,
is the main counterbalance
to the arched form of the
dancer. The backward tilt of
his head is stopped by the
letter 'a'. The drawn letters
are in a strong contrast to
the lithe body of the
dancer holding a
diaphanous veil of wire
screen. They seem to
belong more to the world of
the background shapes, yet
they transcend it and so
enter the dancer's space - a
device which integrates
type and photograph.

LETTERING AND DESIGN
Koeweiden/Postma,
Rotterdam
PHOTOGRAPHY
Hans Verschuuren
CLIENT Dansproduktie

In this same period, traditional and indigenous styles were being lost all over the world. The Industrial Revolution in Europe and the United States divorced many people from the land and destroyed the guild structures that nurtured a living tradition of style derived from necessary craftsmanship. When these traditions had gone, the organic process of stylistic development that had characterized the whole history of art was at an end. By the end of the nineteenth century, the Western urban landscape was a jumble of historical styles addressed to a public that was increasingly fragmented into diverse cultural and socio-economic groups. The seeds of the market survey were planted in this period.

An important response to this phenomen of style was the development of Modernism at the turn of the century. Modernism abandoned revived historical styles and all ornamentation; it rejected the network of associations and historical meanings presumed to reside in the diverse styles of the past and replaced it with a stylistic language derived from the dominant social and economic force of the day: industry.

The ideals of the new movement are best represented by the Bauhaus and the New Typography, both of which began in the 1920s. The new style was characterized by clean lines, a lack of ornamentation and an emphasis on structure. Industrial materials and processes were used frankly. The last traces of the calligraphic origins of Western letterforms were removed from newly designed typefaces. The new style was intended to signify the rise of the worker and the end of class divisions within industrial society.

With hindsight it is clear that the workers' revolution did not unify society under the banner of progress through technology. Rather, the twentieth century has seen society and therefore taste become ever more diversified. The Modernist aesthetic has survived - flourished even - but it did not succeed in eliminating the emotive historical styles of the nineteenth century. Modernism, like the Zen art that influenced it, has a severe aesthetic that appeals only to some sections of the public. Its harmony of proportions and the perfect finish provided by mechanical processes have remained esoteric qualities. Many people in the twentieth century, and throughout the world, share a preference for colour, ornament and rich design. And so Modernism has been joined by a seemingly limitless host of styles - ethnic, nostalgic, counter-

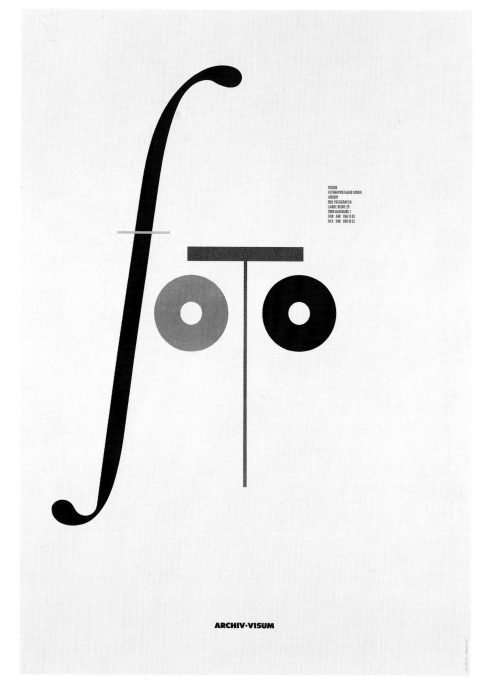

Advertisement for a Photo Archive

Letterforms can be used on their own to build striking compositions. Here hand-drawn letters and Adrian Frutiger's Univers produce a simple concept. The 'O's can be seen as camera lenses or as the eyes of a face, of which the long and graceful 'f' is both shadow and hair. The words 'Archiv-Visum' below are a tight-lipped mouth. But the composition need not be read like this: the shapes of the letters comment on each other in a purely formal way as well. The reduction of the palette to a few rich grey tones reminds us of the great artistic tradition of the black and white photograph.

LETTERING AND DESIGN
Ott + Stein, Berlin
CLIENT Visum Photographic
Archive, Hamburg

culture, historic, classic and all the rest. Graphic designers frequently specialize in particular styles and therefore distinct sectors of the design market: lettering artists cannot generally afford that luxury, and must be able to work in a broad range of styles. Historically, style was a formal environment within which artists and craftsmen worked. In the twentieth century the best designers have turned style into an articulate means of communication.

Establishing a design concept

Hans Rudolf Lutz, formerly of the Schule für Gestaltung (Design School) in Zürich has coined the phrase 'Gestaltung ist auch Information': design is also information. We read designs as surely as we read the text they contain. The designer must not only select the letterforms that convey the appropriate emotions and associations: he must also combine them with other elements such as illustrations or photographs in compositions that convey the right message to the intended audience.

As with the selection of lettering styles, the designer may begin by making a simple statement of his intentions: what is the message to be communicated? Only then can he or she decide how the message can be sent. When the designer's intentions are clear, it is common to produce a thumbnail sketch - or several sketches - suggesting the placement and relative importance of the various elements of a composition. For a composition to work, a hierarchy of elements must be established. The most important element in the hierarchy can be a photograph, an abstract shape, an illustration or a group of letterforms.

If the design is made up entirely of letterforms, then the elements of the composition will be the abstract shapes and counterspaces of the letters themselves. Specific shapes or counterspaces need to be designated as the focal point of the composition. If photographic imagery or illustrations are also included, their relationship to lettering and typography must be determined. Letterforms and images may be integrated or kept separate, but in any case a hierarchy must be established in the composition.

The style and weight of lettering depends on its importance in the hierarchy and on its placement. Very lightweight letters are often difficult to read when positioned over complex imagery. If lettering is being undertaken by a specialist, the designer or art director will need to indicate where his or her work will go so that letterforms can be

Experimental Typography
Roman and italic 'Qs' from the typeface Foundry Wilson, designed by Freda Sack and David Quay, were the basis of this 1991 design. Coloured films applied to a backing board were cut using Ikarus software and an Aristo drafting machine. The first 'Q' was cut and the surrounding film peeled away; a second colour film was applied over this and the second 'Q' cut. When the film surrounding this letter was peeled away, a design of two overlapping letters in three colours was revealed.

LETTERING AND DESIGN
Freda Sack, London

73

8·8·8
年 月 日

為了廿一世紀的香港
三越尖沙咀隆重開店

**Poster for a Hong Kong
Department Store**
Pure joy in calligraphy flows
from this poster by Koichi
Sato, designed to advertise
the opening of a Japanese
department store in Hong
Kong in 1988. The hand-
drawn image consists of a
dynamic contrast between
the irradiated calligraphy,
which cuts a rhythmic
diagonal across the poster,
and the solid block of '8's
which give the conveniently
chosen opening date for
the new store. Airbrushing
was used to achieve the
halation effect around the
letters. The texturing of the
red background with
splattered paint allows the
calligraphy to move
effortlessly in space.

LETTERING AND DESIGN
Koichi Sato, Tokyo
CLIENT Mitsukoshi

MITSUKOS
尖沙咀

produced with the appropriate weight, shape and sense of movement. It is always possible to reduce or enlarge lettering to fit, but adding or subtracting weight is not so easy. Not only the weight and movement of letterforms but also their colour may determine their place in the hierarchy of a composition.

Compositional devices

Visual impact, the most basic device for gaining attention, may be compared with volume in music. But just as a sound can only be described as loud in comparison with other sounds, so the visual impact of a poster or magazine cover is determined by the context in which the image is seen.

It is not always the largest or most boldly coloured letterforms that draw the viewer's eye. In a context of brash, loud posters, an elegant design involving sophisticated colours and letterforms will speak eloquently to a sophisticated audience. And the grammar of style is constantly changing. Visual impact can be achieved only through an awareness of the context of a design.

Amongst the great variety of other ways in which lettering can communicate is, first, visual reference. Letterforms can evoke concepts and associations that emphasize the meaning of a design. The advertisements designed for Smirnoff Vodka by Why Not Associates (page 64), for example, refer to the Constructivist movement in early twentieth-century Russian art. For anyone the letterforms are filled with visual excitement; but to some, the reference will be clear.

A second means of effective communication can be narrative. The message of a design can unfold or develop, revealing either a story or a series of visual relationships. The narrative technique engages the intellect and curiosity of the viewer and uses it to convey a message by degrees. Essential to the media of film and television, narrative techniques are also used increasingly in designs for print. Advertising campaigns may employ a series of posters or other devices to unfold their message, as in the posters designed by BurgerMüllerBauer (page 86) for the Ruhrfestspiele in Recklinghausen (a left-wing cultural festival).

Third, letterforms may be designed to represent objects or ideas, or may contain images such as drawings or photographs. They may also be worked into images using hand, camera or computer techniques. The LP cover designs for Heidi Berry by Chris Bigg of V23 (page 56) integrate

Sculpture

The experimental work of Takenobu Igarashi transforms the two-dimensional forms of letters and numbers into what might be described as graphic sculpture'. In this 1991 piece the number '10' is constructed of precision-cut fibreboard. The sculpture is a three-dimensional puzzle composed of layered shapes that comment on the basic forms of the numbers in the way that a musical fugue comments on a central melody.

LETTERING AND DESIGN
Takenobu Igarashi, Tokyo
CLIENT
Richard Saul Wurman

lettering and imagery to produce complex multimedia effects, though it is worth noting that this is done without the aid of digital technology.

Humour and irony, and other responses such as surprise and nostalgia, are a further means of establishing contact with the viewer. The brightly coloured letters designed by Margaret Horrocks and Jane Wyatt for the 1991 BBC television Christmas season moved and changed on the screen in a humorous way (page 136). The effect helped to identify the station as a source of Christmas cheer.

A fifth tool to engage attention is the use of code: in many designs the viewer must unravel or decode obscure or partly legible letterforms. This technique, now widely used, requires the viewer to supply the necessary information from his or her own memory, thus reinforcing product identity. A series of advertisements designed by Collett, Dickenson and Pearce show the letters of the words Benson and Hedges scattered at random over a still life composed of irrelevant objects. The design style identifies the product immediately; nevertheless, it is difficult to resist the temptation to search out the letters of the name. The concept is an inspired solution to the problems posed by legal restrictions on the content of cigarette advertisements.

Technical considerations

Any decision concerning the placement of lettering in a composition must take into account the techniques by which the letterforms and other elements will be created. One rule of thumb in the design profession is, 'Don't design anything you can't produce'. There are over fifty techniques for the production and reproduction of lettering represented in this book (see the Design of Letters section), showing that virtually anything is possible. But in order to decide which technique is appropriate, there are always several factors to be considered: first, the function of the letters; second, the technology available to make them; third, their style; fourth, whether the letters will be made in-house or by a specialist; fifth, how they will be integrated with the other elements of the design; and finally, the budget and production schedule. For one job the budget may weigh heavily in the design process; for another the demands of legibility may restrict the forms of the letters that can be used. The style of lettering originally selected may even have to change if it cannot be produced or paid for. All six factors are balanced against the others in the process.

LOW TO MIDDLE TAR As defined by H.M.Government
Warning: SMOKING CAN CAUSE HEART DISEASE Health Departments' Chief Medical Officers

Cigarette Advertisement
The introduction of laws in the UK restricting tobacco advertisements gave rise to a new generation of advertising techniques. One of the most famous campaigns to result was that of 1986 for Benson and Hedges by Collett, Dickenson, Pearce and Partners. The product identity has been reinforced by making the public search for the product name in images with no direct relation to smoking. Here its costituent letters join other letters among the 'stubble' floating on the surface of shaving foam. The gold box to the left remains easily identifiable despite being clean-shaven. The sharp if irrelevant wit of the advertisement subtly assigns a certain intelligence to the product itself.

LETTERING AND DESIGN
Nigel Rose for Collett, Dickenson, Pearce and Partners Ltd, London
CLIENT Gallaher

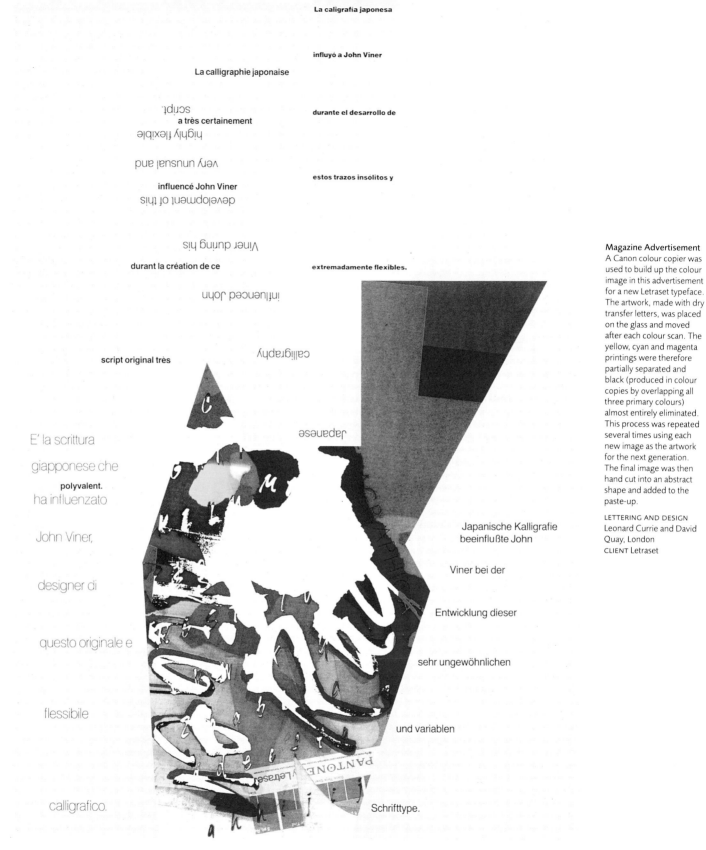

Magazine Advertisement
A Canon colour copier was used to build up the colour image in this advertisement for a new Letraset typeface. The artwork, made with dry transfer letters, was placed on the glass and moved after each colour scan. The yellow, cyan and magenta printings were therefore partially separated and black (produced in colour copies by overlapping all three primary colours) almost entirely eliminated. This process was repeated several times using each new image as the artwork for the next generation. The final image was then hand cut into an abstract shape and added to the paste-up.

LETTERING AND DESIGN
Leonard Currie and David Quay, London
CLIENT Letraset

Lettering as Image

Logos

The special place occupied by the logo in the field of hand- lettering merits particular attention here. A logo is a composition in miniature that serves to identify a corporation, institution, event or product. Logo design is one of the most difficult tasks required of graphic designers and lettering artists. Modern corporate culture requires that most logos be utterly simple, devoid of unnecessary elements and ornament. They must be capable of use in several sizes and on a variety of materials. They must also contribute to the success of the businesses and products that they serve to identify and so be the embodiment of professionalism, perfect in design and execution.

Because a logo must send out a clear and confident message, its design begins by establishing with perfect clarity the one idea to be communicated. This idea may be included in the designer's brief, but he or she may be required to work with the client to define the message.

In most cases a designer will experiment with each of three basic possibilities in an attempt to find the most forceful vehicle for what must be communicated. Letterforms alone may be used: hand-drawn, typeset, manipulated type or a combination of type and hand-lettering. They may be legible or depend for recognition on their characteristic shape and composition. Alternatively, a designer may opt for illustration alone, or thirdly, a combination of letterforms and illustration. This book, of course, celebrates those logos which incorporate letterforms in particular.

In general, type and mechanically produced forms convey a sense of authority. The more hand-made the forms appear to be, the more they tend to convey a sense of human warmth, intimacy and immediacy. The emotional groupings made in section one of this book should remind readers of the less verbal connotations of various lettering styles. However, in choosing letterforms for logos, designers need to remember that they are perhaps the most intense concentration of form and content in the world of commercial design.

Limited Edition Book
The ability of present-day designers to see letterforms as potentially the sole elements of a design is based on developments in twentieth-century art. The German artist Josua Reichert began experimenting with compositions of letters in the '60s. Here the Cyrillic letter 'L' is built into an architectonic still life. The book from which this image is taken, produced in 1967, contains one composition for each letter of the Russian alphabet. Reichert claims it is a fairy-tale of Cyrillic letters.

LETTERING AND DESIGN
Josua Reichert

Logo

This logo was designed by David Quay in 1985 to serve as the mast-head for the in-house magazine of a firm of colour-separation and plate-making specialists. The logo was produced using several plate-making and colour-separation technologies, as well as symbolic representations of electronic and creative techniques, including calligraphy, computer generated characters, a bit-mapped 'D', a laser-scanned 'A', a hand-drawn 'H' and a printer's registration mark.

LETTERING AND DESIGN
David Quay, London
CLIENT Ad-Plates, Ltd.

Three Pentagram Logos

Logos are twentieth-century heraldry, serving as battle standards in the fight for profit. Pentagram have produced some of the most effective and elegant logos of the last thirty years. These are often powerful distillations of corporate image and style. Presented here are three examples that consist entirely of manipulated letterforms. Each plays with concepts of space in a unique way. Their full force is realized in an interplay of black and white.

1 LETTERING AND DESIGN
Mervyn Kurlansky and Lora Starling, London
CLIENT Shiseido Ltd
DATE 1977
2 LETTERING AND DESIGN
Colin Forbes, London
CLIENT Designers and Art Directors Association
DATE 1962
3 LETTERING AND DESIGN
John McConnell and Laurence Dunmore, London
CLIENT Stanhope
DATE 1987

1   2   3

Exhibition Poster
The building-block 'S' used as the central image on this 1989 exhibition poster by Shin Matsunaga serves in various guises as the corporate identity for his design firm. Unusually perhaps, the logo of a Japanese designer is based on a Latin rather than a Japanese character, yet the simple geometry of the letter announces its national origins. In its black and white versions this computer-drawn logo is closer to the *mon* used to identify the aristocratic families of feudal Japan than to the original Latin character.

LETTERING AND DESIGN
Shin Matsunaga
CLIENT Daiichishiko Co Ltd

1

Newspaper Banner
Logo for a Hotel
In these two designs of 1978 and 1980, Hassan Massoudi has combined ancient and modern styles of Arabic calligraphy. Massoudi's translation of the *Le Monde* banner into Arabic was drawn by hand and incorporated hatched drop-shadows identical to those on the original, thus ensuring the instant recognition of the French daily on the news stand.

2

The circular design incorporates ancient Kufic letterforms with modern geometric forms to produce a logo for the Al Mutres Hotel. The circular format is itself a traditional one. The logo therefore conveys a dual image of old-world hospitality and modern efficiency.

1 LETTERING AND DESIGN
Hassan Massoudi, Paris
CLIENT *Le Monde*

2 LETTERING AND DESIGN
Hassan Massoudi, Paris
CLIENT Frantel Hotels

PARKETT

International Childrens Festival 1990

Logo Design
The avant-garde art journal *Parkett* rejected all conventional styles of corporate logo as trendy, institutional-looking and reminiscent of advertising and graphic design. The artist Enzo Cucchi suggested that someone's grandmother should do an embroidered rendition instead. In 1984 Bice Curiger designed the letters and her mother, Mama Livia Curiger, embroidered them in linen. The embroidery is a suitable metaphor for art: it is hand-made, reveals the process of its making and is timeless.

DESIGN Bice Curiger, Zürich
EMBROIDERY
Mama Livia Curiger
CLIENT: Parkett-Verlag, AG

Logo for an International Festival
Julian Waters' mastery of the calligraphic line conveys a sense of fresh energy within the often conventional boundaries of corporate style. The flourishes and curves of this logo for the 1990 International Children's Festival are vibrant and inhesitating, yet still impart a sense of authority.

LETTERING Julian Waters, Washington DC
ART DIRECTION Celia Stratton, Washington DC
CLIENT National Park Service, Washington DC

Book Title
The sense of immediacy often achieved by calligraphy can also be obtained in other ways. This book title by Shin Matsunaga, undertaken in 1977, relies on the uneven impression of wood display type to evoke the feeling of early block-printed posters and public notices.

LETTERING AND DESIGN
Shin Matsunaga, Tokyo
CLIENT Kodansha Ltd

Self Promotion
This copperplate logo was drawn by Leonard Currie in 1990 using a scratch pen dipped in India ink. The inspiration for the piece came from the 1743 edition of George Bickham's *The Universal Penman*. The luxuriant thicks and thins owe their inspiration to Victorian models.

LETTERING AND DESIGN
Leonard Currie, London

Logo
The original for this 1990 logo was written on rice paper and unretouched. As anyone who has worked with ink on rice paper will realize, there is no room for doubt or hesitation: if the pen stops moving, blots form at once. This design is impressive for the confidence of the letterforms, achieved despite the speed of execution.

LETTERING AND DESIGN
John Stevens, East Meadow, New York
ART DIRECTION
Larry Fremantle
CLIENT Atlantic Records

GOOD LIVING SHOW '91
TOKYO INTERNATIONAL GOOD LIVING SHOW '91 · Tokyo International Trade Fair Commission
APRIL 26→MAY 1,1991 / HARUMI TOKYO

In Pursuit of Rich, Easy and Comfortable Housing
ゆとり快適実感

Exhibition Poster

In Koichi Sato's 1982 poster, the numbers one to ten appear in both their Japanese and Arabic forms and are accompanied by the corresponding number of three-dimensional objects. Thus a typographic Japanese '8' is overlaid by a calligraphic Arabic '8'; to the side are eight tiny seashells. The opalescent numbers are surrounded by the halo characteristic of Koichi Sato's style. The golden gradation effect was achieved by computer.

LETTERING AND DESIGN
Koichi Sato, Tokyo
CLIENT Takeo Co Ltd

'91グッドリビングショー▲
平成3年4月26日(金)〜5月1日(水)
東京国際見本市会場(晴海)

Poster

A monogram of the letters 'G' and 'L' serves to illustrate this poster designed by Shin Matsunaga for the 1990 Good Living Show, held in Tokyo. The letters are treated as flat planes of colour that are superimposed and manipulated to suggest architecture: the two-dimensional forms contain a hint of the third dimension.

LETTERING AND DESIGN
Shin Matsunaga, Tokyo
CLIENT Good Living Show

Calendar

Italo Lupi boldly penetrates the viewer's space with this Egyptian 'A' for August in a 1991 calendar. The hand-drawn letter appears to be a monumental form standing on a rose-coloured ground, its edges textured to resemble cut stone. The warm colours and oblique shadow suggest the sunlight of late summer.

LETTERING Sandro Farina and Ivo Waldburger in collaboration with Italo Lupi, Milan
DESIGN AND ART DIRECTION Italo Lupi, Milan
CLIENT Grafiche Mariano Tipografia

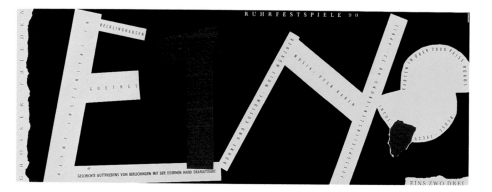

Series of Posters for a Cultural Festival

The colours of the German flag have been called into service on this series of posters for a left-wing cultural festival in 1990. The large letterforms and other shapes were made by cutting and tearing paper; type was superimposed at the next stage. Though letters are used here as abstract shapes in dynamic compositions, they remain entirely legible. The message is clear: alternative letterforms, like alternative cultural statements, do not have to be unintelligible.

LETTERING Rainer Bauer, Pfintztal, Germany
DESIGN BurgerMüllerBauer, Pfintztal, Germany
CLIENT Ruhrfestspiele Recklinghausen

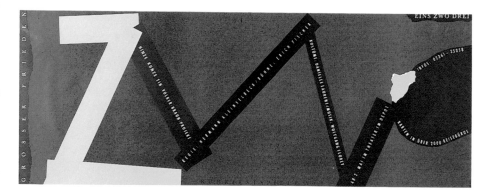

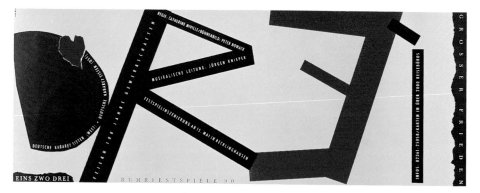

Limited Edition Print
Toshiyasu Nanbu created
this typographic puzzle for
a special exhibition held in
Tokyo in 1988. The piece
was produced on the
photocopier. Typographic
letterforms were
transferred on to acetate to
allow them to be reversed,
layered and partially
obscured by overlapping.
The black background was
textured by means of a
rough-grade tint. The result
is an image that compels us
to decode its fragmented
message but at the same
time makes this impossible.

LETTERING AND DESIGN
Toshiyasu Nanbu, Osaka

Greetings Card
For this greetings card,
produced in 1989, Italo
Lupi turned to an
eighteenth-century
alphabet composed of
figural silhouettes. These
represent folk in various
stages of work and merry-
making. Italo Lupi has
simply added splashes of
transparent colour that
might be seen as confetti,
balloons or lanterns, the
latter, of course,
appropriate to the client.

DESIGN AND ART DIRECTION
Italo Lupi, Milan
CLIENT Flos Lighting

Limited Edition Book
Hans-Joachim Burgert has
used calligraphy and home-
spun typefaces in an
extensive series of limited
edition books. In this 1987
treatment of the story of the
prophet Jonah, Burgert
combines calligraphy and
hand-coloured drawings,
the two perfectly integrated
without losing legibility.

LETTERING AND DESIGN
Hans-Joachim Burgert,
Berlin

Limited Edition Book
The German Hans Schmidt
is one of the most influential
lettering artists of the
twentieth-century. His
work concentrates on
discovering the essential
forms of letters. In this
hand-printed book
produced in 1964, the
letterforms are reduced to
semi-circles, rectangles and
triangles. Contrasts of
weight or texture are
achieved through colour
and the use of variable
pressure when stamping
the wooden blocks on the
paper.

LETTERING AND DESIGN
Hans Schmidt, Baden Hard,
Germany

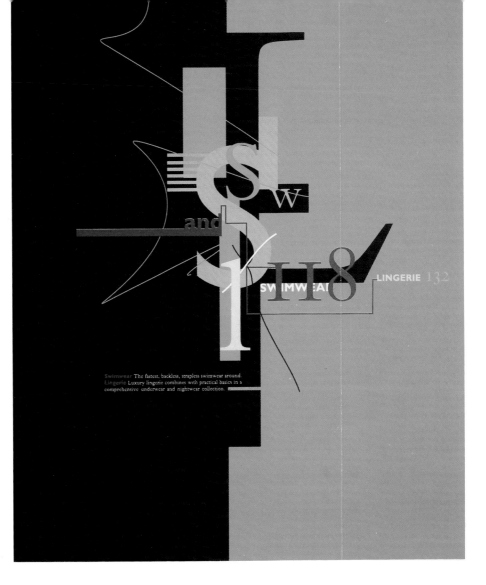

Swimwear The fastest, backless, strapless swimwear around.
Lingerie Luxury lingerie combines with practical basics in a
comprehensive underwear and nightwear collection.

Directory

The abstract qualities of letterforms can be used to produce decorative elements in books and magazines. Medieval illuminated manuscripts often relied on decorated initials, sometimes covering entire pages, for ornament; these ornaments also served to identify important divisions in the text. This section divider from the seventh *Next Directory* serves precisely this purpose. The composition of letterforms is entirely ornamental, and the jewel-like colours are strongly reminiscent of Romanesque illuminations.

LETTERING AND DESIGN
Why Not Associates,
London
CLIENT *Next Directory*

PIETER NOOTEN / MICHAEL BROOK

SLEEPS WITH THE FISHES

L.P. CAD715 / C.D. CAD715CD

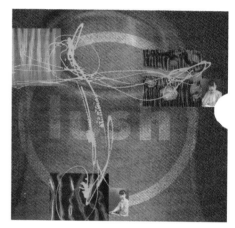

Magazine Advertisement
An alphabet of sound was created by Paul Elliman in 1991 for a series of advertisements for The Cornflake Shop, a London sound-systems store. The vocal components of several words were performed by Angela Taylor in a photo-booth. Thus, each photograph represents a sound, and the viewer must reproduce the gesture in order to discover what sound is indicated.

DESIGN Paul Elliman, London
LETTERING ARTIST Angela Taylor
CLIENT The Cornflake Shop

Album Cover
Chris Bigg of V23 is widely known for the highly personal style of his calligraphic marks. The design for this album cover of 1987 relies entirely on the unique qualities of the eccentric red mark, which glows through a spot varnish on a matt black ground and is flanked by tiny yellow symbols connected by arcing lines that resemble the schematic diagrams used to describe dance steps. The relationship between these symbols and the calligraphic mark is a mystery that, it is implied, can be fathomed only be listening to the album.

LETTERING Chris Bigg, London
DESIGN AND ART DIRECTION Vaughan Oliver at V23, London
CLIENT 4AD Records

CD Cover
The strange and irrational quality of this calligraphic mark is a fitting comment on the surreal group of images. Unlike the more conventional calligraphy seen elsewhere in this book, this 1990 piece expresses the decadent aesthetic promoted by many designers working for the music industry. Three pairs of images - antique tinted photographs and squares of organic inspiration - are linked by the calligraphy, which runs over the typographic word 'Lush' and a photographically distorted fingertip.

LETTERING Chris Bigg, London
DESIGN AND ART DIRECTION Vaughan Oliver and Chris Bigg at V23, London
PHOTOGRAPHY Jim Friedman
CLIENT 4AD Records

Single Cover

Calligraphic marks may suggest irrational or decadent concepts, or, equally well, a sense of energy and movement. This 1989 single cover displays calligraphy by Ruth Rowland that retains legibility while suggesting something of its vibrant contents.

LETTERING Ruth Rowland, London
DESIGN David Crow
CLIENT Island Records

Album Cover

The expressive potential of Arabic calligraphy was explored much earlier than that of Western calligraphy. As a result, distortions of the basic letterforms rarely affect legibility as strongly as they would where the Latin alphabet is concerned. This Arabic calligraphy by Ruth Rowland is conventional in form and style and remains highly legible.

LETTERING Ruth Rowland, London
DESIGN David Crow, London
CLIENT Island Records

Album Cover

A globe of glowing plastic is surrounded by Saturn-like rings bearing the letters of the word 'Pixies' in this piece by Vaughan Oliver of V23. The design refers directly to lettering styles of the Art Deco period and so carries connotations of polished chrome diners and deco picture palaces.

LETTERING AND DESIGN Vaughan Oliver of V23, London
CLIENT The Pixies

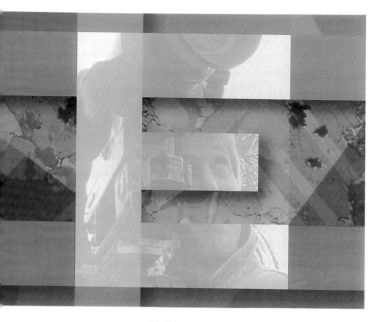

Television Sequence

Morgan Sendall has used letterforms as the basis for multimedia images in this 1992 sequence for Thames Television. Employing Quantel Paintbox and Harry, Morgan Sendall has integrated photographic imagery with abstract colour and textural elements, all within the outlines of simple sans-serif captials. The palette has been softened and includes only pastels and greys, thus lending a muted and decorative quality to the lettering. Though the sequence clearly reveals high-tech methods of production, each letter considered on its own resembles a painted image.

LETTERING AND DESIGN
Morgan Sendall, London
CLIENT David Fair for
Thames Television

Television Advertisements

Subtle typographic manipulations are often the best way to produce a strong identity. Using Freehand on the Mac, Jonathan Barnbrook simply extended the central bar of the Garamond 'E' to form an arrow in this series of television advertisements produced in 1991 for Britain's Nuclear Electric. The images and type were integrated on Harry by David Hughes.

LETTERING Jonathan
Barnbrook, London
DESIGN David May and
Jonathan Barnbrook,
London
ART DIRECTION David May
of J. Walter Thompson,
London
ANIMATION David Lodge
CLIENT Nuclear Electric

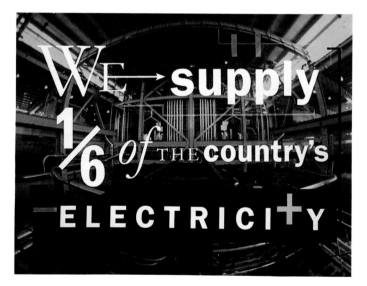

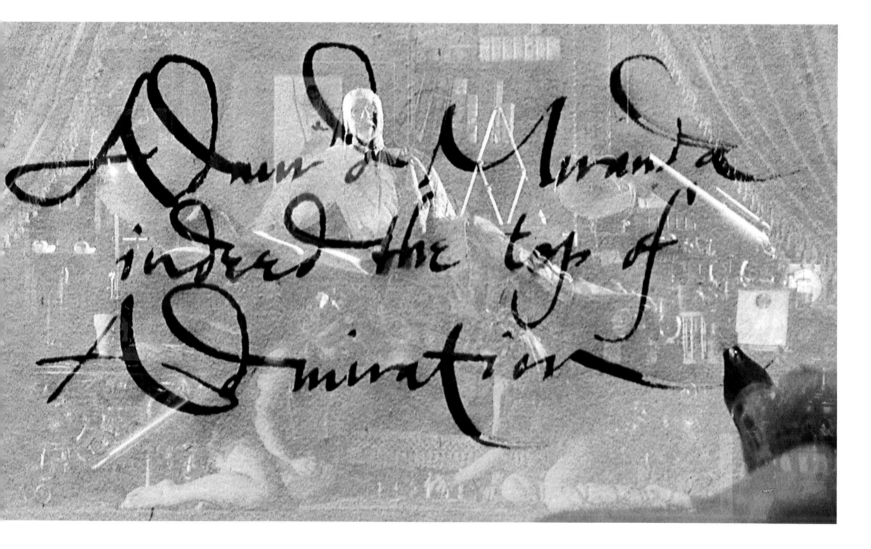

Lettering for Film
Calligraphy runs like a
continuous thread through
Peter Greenaway's 1991
film *Prospero's Books*.
Greenaway conceived his
version of Shakespeare's
play *The Tempest* as an
exploration of the
relationships of man to
knowledge and books.
Throughout, Prospero
writes the play that he
himself acts and lives.
Calligraphy appears in
many forms: written swiftly
with a quill, manipulated on
Paintbox to resemble
advancing flames and
blended into complex
multimedia images. The
credits and printed
advertisements also used
calligraphy.

The style of the writing was
derived from what little is
known of Shakespeare's
own hand, though at
different stages of the film
the letterforms were made
to express the dominant
feeling or to fit in particular
spaces.

LETTERING
Brody Neuenschwander,
Bruges, Belgium
DIRECTOR Peter Greenaway

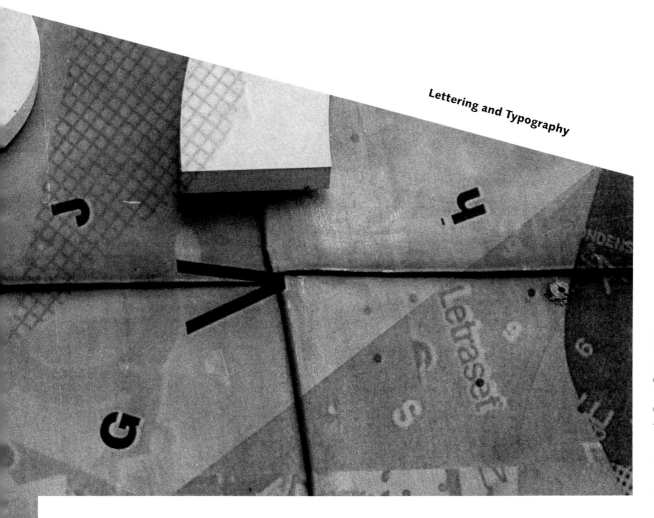

Experimental Lettering
The number 87 in this
image, observed by
Leonard Currie on a London
building, was shot on slide
film using a hand-held
camera. A second 35 mm
slide shot from randomly
placed dry transfer letters
and textures, was placed in
the same slide frame as the
architectural image. The
combination of two- and
three-dimensional images,
the latter showing washed-
out colours, produces a
surreal world of fixed and
floating characters.

LETTERING AND DESIGN
Leonard Currie, London

Lettering and Typography

The type historian Beatrice Ward described typography as a 'crystal goblet ... fit to hold the vintage of the human mind'. Most typographers and graphic designers would argue, however, that type is rarely the crystal-clear vessel that Ward claims it should be. Text faces speak a subtle language of style that gives visual emphasis to verbal content, while display faces can produce compositions charged with emotion; but it is indeed rare for type to produce the emotional and compositional impact of hand-lettering. Type, after all, is generally designed for use in a variety of situations. Legibility must be built into the letters, and this exerts a restraining influence on their forms. Hand-lettering, by contrast, is made for specific applications and can rely for legibility largely on context. A freer development of form is therefore possible.

The contrast in the ways that type and hand-lettering work makes them ideal partners in graphic design: together they can achieve maximum expressive value and total legibility. This potential, combined with the ease with which hand-lettering can now be worked into designs for print, will ensure an increasingly important role for hand-lettering in designs involving type.

Bringing lettering and type together

How can hand-lettering and type co-exist in a design, what lettering styles are best suited to a particular typeface and how is sufficient contrast ensured within a harmonious design? The formal characteristics of letterforms are each capable of manipulation: shape, weight, size, slope, colour, texture, edge, entasis (gradual thickening or thinning of the main parts of letters), serifs and decorative elements such as dropped shadows and in-lines can be adapted to produce letterforms that sit well with a given typeface, as well as conveying the desired formal and emotional qualities. Built up element by element, letterforms can achieve an effective level of harmony and contrast. For example, if a typeface has classical proportions, bracketed serifs and no slope, it might be paired with an italic letter with similarly classical proportions, pen-made serifs but pronounced slope. Other contrasts could be achieved through colour, size and texture. The hand-lettering and the type would share certain features - classical proportions and serifs - and contrast in others - slope, size, colour and texture. The more elements of contrast built into the combination, the more jarring the effect.

99

Exhibition Poster

The pairing of hand-lettering and type requires the careful balancing of formal harmonies and contrasts. Ott + Stein here selected Univers to accompany the simple geometric letters of the words 'Design/Dasein' (Design/Presence). The sans serif and monoline forms of Univers harmonize with the rectangles, triangles and other shapes of the drawn lettering, holding the design together, but the semi-circular forms of the hand-lettering contrast with the squarish ellipses of Frutiger's typeface. This allows the type to be tightly packed to produce vertical emphasis. The vertical rectangle of grey type then provides a base on which the tilted square of hand-lettering can balance. A typeface derived from circular forms would have interfered with this central motif and produced a square rather than a rectangular block of text, destroying the dynamism of the composition.

LETTERING AND DESIGN
Ott + Stein, Berlin
CLIENT Museum für Kunst und Gewerbe, Hamburg

An analysis of the stylistic characteristics of the major type families highlights how points of harmony and contrast can be produced in hand-lettering when used in conjuction with type. It should facilitate a choice of typeface to go, for example, with an elegant and heavily flourished copperplate letter written directly with a steel pen, or make it possible to design a title for a feature article on Mozart to fit with the cover style of a long-established news weekly.

Guidelines for commissioning tailor-made lettering are given in the directory at the end of this book. Although the creation of a design cannot follow a pre-determined plan, it is often best to begin by determining the general look of the design, including the hand lettering, and to proceed from there to the selection of the appropriate typefaces. Most designers will have a wide range of type catalogues in the studio but may not have a selection of hand-lettering examples to refer to. Generally, it is easier to produce hand-lettering that agrees in style with a typeface than to find a typeface that suits the unique features of an example of hand-lettering. Other considerations may, however, determine the order of working. A briefing between a lettering artist and designer may be necessary before any final type decision can be made. At the very least this brief should specify the shape and size of the space to be filled, the style, emotional message and associations to be communicated by the lettering and the overall design, the movement and directional sense required, the level of legibility, and the other elements of the design to which the lettering must respond.

Old-style faces such as Bembo and Times are characterized by classical proportions, bracketed serifs and a gradual transition from thick to thin elements with calligraphic weighting. Capitals are usually slightly shorter than ascenders, and there is occasional entasis. With their calligraphic basis and classical proportions and spacing, they display balanced horizontal and vertical stresses. The relationship of black to white is also balanced, giving a timeless feeling of elegance and stability in the best examples.

Such faces were first developed under the influence of the broad pen. As products of the Renaissance and Baroque, they witnessed the transition from broad-pen italics to the earliest pressure-made copper-

Exhibition Poster
This 1987 poster announces an exhibition on the novelist Natsume Soseki held in a Tokyo department store. Kazumasa Nagai has placed the four characters of the novelist's name at the corners of the poster, set in bold type and filled with patterns taken from the covers of notebooks and diaries belonging to the novelist. This simple typographic manipulation would be meaningful to a Japanese audience familiar with the source of the decorative patterns.

LETTERING AND DESIGN
Kazumasa Nagai, Tokyo
CLIENT Isetan Department Store

plate scripts; thus traditional calligraphic lettering displaying a rational distribution of weight would obviously harmonize most closely with old-style types - see especially the work of John Stevens, Julian Waters and Georgia Deaver, for example. Scrawls, random marks and eccentric letterforms, on the other hand, would have little in common with this family and might be useful where strong dissonance is required.

Transitional and modern faces such as Baskerville, Modern Extended and Bodoni display fuller proportions than old-style faces; these faces generally have unbracketed serifs, an abrupt transition from thick to thin and a vertical distribution of weight that is un-calligraphic. This vertical stress can lead to a condensed look despite the generous proportions. Though their proportions are not dramatically different from old-style faces, the vertical weighting and strong horizontal look produced by the unbracketed serifs make for text blocks with a grid-like quality. There is a stronger sense of geometry and black-white contrast than in old-style faces.

The first transitional faces are contemporary with copperplate writing at its height. Eighteenth- and nineteenth-century calligraphy and lettering are frequently heavily flourished and often display eccentric forms and decorations, while in the age of the signwriter the exuberance of the Victorian display face was characteristic. Classical balance gives way to the power and urgency of the Industrial Revolution.

Hand-lettering, in order to harmonize with transitional and modern faces, would need to show abrupt transitions from thick to thin strokes, strong vertical or horizontal emphasis and a distribution of weight that does not conform to the logic of the broad pen; hence the work of Chris Bigg, Margot Chase and Ruth Rowland is especially appropriate. Traditional and modern faces also combine well with imagery and are thus good partners for letterforms worked into shapes, colours, photographs or illustrations. Typefaces such as Bodoni and Walbaum retain a modern and technical feel despite their origins in the early nineteenth century.

Egyptian faces such as Rockwell and Calvert are essentially modern faces with slab serifs and virtually no thick and thin elements. They therefore have no calligraphic basis, but convey a

Limited Edition Book
It is occasionally necessary to produce hand-drawn forms of a typographic nature in order to harmonize completely with calligraphic letterforms. This screen-printed book undertaken by Susan Skarsgard in 1989 combines elegant Roman capitals with flowing and only partially legible calligraphy. The Romans have precisely the right weight and feeling of movement, a difficult achievement as, though few can judge the quality of informal calligraphy, our general familiarity with type makes us critical judges of formal Roman capitals.

LETTERING AND DESIGN
Susan Skarsgard, Ann Arbor, Michigan
BINDING Julia Miller

Poster

The difficulty of integrating calligraphy and type is neatly overcome in this poster of 1990: Werner Schneider has used his own calligraphy and his own typeface (Schneider-Antiqua). The two elements therefore have a sympathy that is often lacking where hand-lettering and type are brought together from different sources. Schneider's typographic capitals have a pronounced calligraphic basis, displaying an entasis, serif structure and weighting on the curved strokes that derive directly from written forms of the Renaissance. The calligraphy is based on the elegant secretarial hands of the same period.

LETTERING AND DESIGN
Werner Schneider,
Wiesbaden
ART DIRECTION Paul Shaw,
New York
CLIENT The Society of
Scribes Ltd, New York

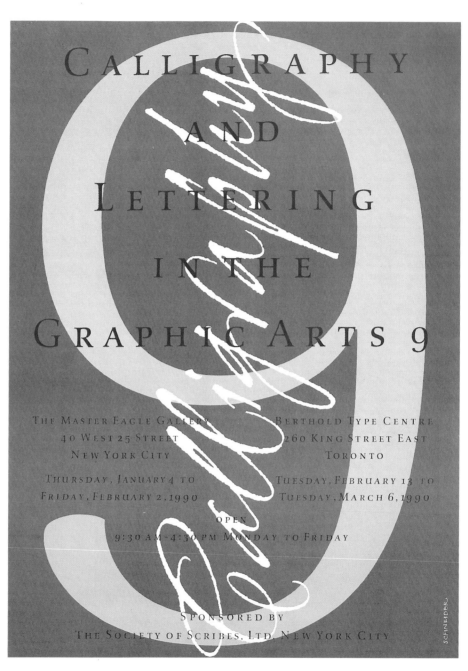

sense of geometrical precision. They produce an even texture with a chunky, solid feel. The black-white contrast is strong but consistent, and well-defined text blocks can be achieved. This family is contemporaneous with modern faces but descends from display rather than text types. Many of these faces have been redesigned in the twentieth century to introduce somewhat more elegant forms.

The solid, mechanical quality of Egyptian faces makes them ideal partners for letters with a strongly geometric style. Letters cut from paper or stamped from simple blocks would harmonize closely with Egyptian type, but powerful brush marks also stand up well to their clear contrasts. The work of Hans Schmidt, Why Not, April Greiman and Shin Matsunaga is all in sympathy with this family, whereas elegant letters with pronounced thick and thin strokes and fluid rhythms would contrast markedly with the solidity of Egyptians. In certain situations this could be desirable: fine calligraphy cut from metal would run beautifully over enlarged Egyptians reverse-cast in concrete or etched in glass.

Although there are important differences between sans serif and grotesque faces, both groups are virtually monoline and geometric rather than calligraphic in inspiration. Sans serif faces are classic in proportions, while grotesques display the generous proportions of Egyptian type. Entasis is uncommon in both families. Grotesques - including Univers, Helvetica and Franklin Gothic, and sans serifs - including Futura, Gill Sans and Optima - both produce even textures. The former have a slight vertical emphasis; the latter tend towards the horizontal. Black and white contrasts vary from the classical balance of Optima to the strong dominance of black in the majority of grotesque faces.

Grotesques developed at the same time as Egyptian type but sans serif faces are products of the twentieth century and so parallel the introduction of photo-lithography and the integration of full-colour imagery and type, and for this reason have been tremendously important in modern design. They have an essential sympathy with the technologies now in use. Their solid, geometric basis allows them to be used as abstract elements in typographic compositions, as can be seen in the work of Ott and Stein. This same abstract quality combines well with random marks, scrawls and handwriting. Broad-

**Promotional Pack
for a Vineyard**
As shown in the Werner Schneider piece opposite, historical considerations can be useful in guiding the pairing of hand-lettering and type. The same is true of Anna Ronchi's combination of an old-style typeface with italic calligraphy in 1991. Old-style faces retain marked traces of their calligraphic origins, and are thus generally suitable for use with broad-pen calligraphy. The calligraphy may be formal or informal, controlled or expressive.

LETTERING AND DESIGN
Anna Ronchi, Milan
CLIENT Carlo Brignolio

Magazine Advertisement
This advertisement by Chris Bigg combines calligraphy, hand-drawn letters and manipulated type. The type was set by photo-composition and splattered with solvents which dissolved the letterforms and caused them to run down the film. All remaining letterforms were drawn or written by hand. This piece was produced for *Emigré* as part of a special edition in 1988 devoted to the work of 4AD.

LETTERING AND DESIGN
Chris Bigg, London
CLIENT *Emigré* Magazine

pen calligraphy is less appropriate, though precisely rendered copperplate works in some cases. Carefully written traditional forms would in most cases produce a feeling of discord when juxtaposed with typefaces of this group.

The preceding analysis of the most important type families and their stylistic sympathies can of necessity be only a general guide; no pairing of type and hand-lettering can ever be ruled out, as demonstrated by the many examples in this book. Experimentation with random pairings of hand-lettering and type over the years helps develop a critical awareness of how the two interact, aided by an examination of the ten elements of letterforms discussed earlier in this section.

Manipulated type

The manipulation of type has become increasingly important in graphic design with the advent of digital technology. Personal and mainframe computers can be used to alter individual forms or entire compositions of type. At the same time designers are constantly discovering new ways of using basic technology, including hand techniques, to manipulate type for specific designs.

Sources of type for manipulation include film-setting, dry-transfer letters, computer print-outs, photocopied or faxed type and type taken from books, magazines, works of art and the street. Letterforms thus obtained can be altered by hand using basic tools such as mechanical pens and brushes, or they can be dissected with the scalpel and reassembled as a paste-up. The photocopier is one of the most versatile manipulative tools: it can be used to harvest letterforms from type catalogues and early printed books, to create astonishing colour effects with omnichrome films, and to distort letterforms by moving them on the glass while a copy is being made. These and many other basic studio techniques are discussed in the Design of Letters section.

Without question, however, the computer has now become the principal tool for the manipulation of type. This book features a wide range of works produced by altering the received forms of type on the computer screen. From the blended letters of Julian Waters to the spun and twisted letters of Takenobu Igarashi, the computer has opened up the printed surface to three-dimensional effects never before applied to letterforms.

Calendar

The number '23' was produced using Adobe Illustrator on the Apple Macintosh. By irradiating the precise geometric forms of the numbers, Mitsuo Katsui has created an inconsistent illusion of depth, and heightened the tension between the positive and negative elements. This concentration on the rich contrasts of black and white places the design firmly within the developing tradition of Japanese calligraphy.

LETTERING AND DESIGN
Mitsuo Katsui, Tokyo
CLIENT Kajima Corporation

Calligraphic and eccentric typefaces

Calligraphic and eccentric typefaces illustrate how the study of calligraphy can yield important insights into the design of type. Also, they show that type - even text type - need not be based on Western the traditions of geometry and legibility.

An examination of calligraphy and the history or writing is an excellent (some would say indispensable) basis for a career in type design. Complex issues of form, spacing, weight and legibility cannot be fully grasped at the fundamental level without coming to terms with the origins of letterforms. Without a sound knowledge of the core principles governing the shapes of any alphabet, it is also difficult to manipulate them in the extravagant and visually powerful ways illustrated in this book. These principles were established in antiquity through a sustained exploration of the formal characteristics of the broad pen and brush. They were fixed in lead in the fifteenth and sixteenth centuries and only eradicated from certain classes of type during the Industrial Revolution. Since then, no set of geometric principles has replaced the simple logic of the broad pen in the design of legible forms. Old-style faces with their calligraphic basis continue to determine the standard of legibility.

The eccentric typefaces and alphabets illustrated in this section, though, are based not on calligraphic principles but on principles of harmony and contrast derived from the fine arts. In many cases they push legibility to the limit, spilling over into the area of codes and cryptic systems and compelling us to extend our concept of the alphabet. As can be seen here, it is the artist's exploration of new forms and meanings that provides the inspiration for the designers and typographers of the future.

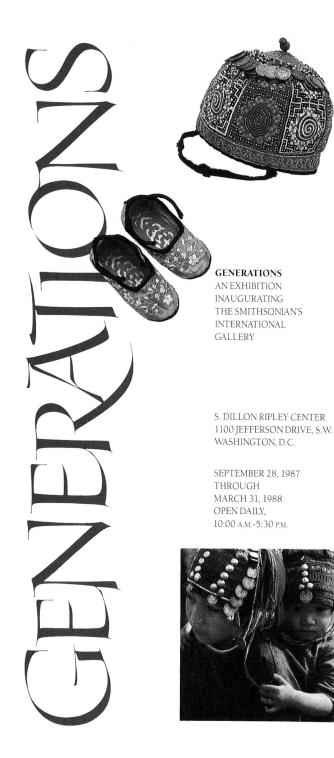

GENERATIONS

GENERATIONS
AN EXHIBITION
INAUGURATING
THE SMITHSONIAN'S
INTERNATIONAL
GALLERY

S. DILLON RIPLEY CENTER
1100 JEFFERSON DRIVE, S.W.
WASHINGTON, D.C.

SEPTEMBER 28, 1987
THROUGH
MARCH 31, 1988
OPEN DAILY,
10:00 A.M.-5:30 P.M.

Exhibition Poster
In order to combine hand-lettering and type, points both of harmony and of contrast must be found. Julian Waters' elegant pen-made capitals share several features with the Berkeley Old Style face that accompanies them. The Berkeley shows calligraphic weighting (the backward tilt of the 'O'), bracketed serifs, entasis and a nearly circular basis for the curved strokes; Julian Waters' calligraphy freely interprets these characteristics. Movement and a variety of serif forms are added as points of contrast.

LETTERING Julian Waters, Washington DC
ART DIRECTION Judy Kirpich, Washington DC
CLIENT Smithsonian Institution
DESIGN Beth Bathe and Judy Kirpich

Magazine Cover
It is not always possible to achieve formal harmony between type and hand-lettering. In the case of magazine covers hand-lettering is often added without reference to the long-established banner style. John Stevens designed the word 'Mozart' for the cover of this 1991 issue of *Newsweek* in order to conjure up the musical splendours of eighteenth-century Austria. The calligraphy sits well with the photographic image and, though arguably not an entirely comfortable match for the type, its letterforms play off the solid Egyptians in an interesting way.

LETTERING John Stevens, East Meadow, New York
DESIGN AND ART DIRECTION Mark Inglis, New York
PHOTOGRAPHY Hans Neleman
CLIENT *Newsweek*

Poster for a Lecture
A sense of depth may help to organize a complex assembly of two- and three-dimensional elements. This poster of 1990 combines photography, graphic symbol and several weights and sizes of Futura. The watery calligraphy by Derick Pao brings a sense of the third dimension to the letterforms. Hand-lettering is seen here to serve on three levels: as symbol, as compositional device and as legible information.

LETTERING Derick Pao, Scarborough, Ontario
DESIGN Ric Riordon and Derick Pao, Toronto, Ontario
ART DIRECTION Ric Riordon
CLIENT Ontario Science Centre, Toronto

Architectural Lettering
The job of combining hand-lettering and type is made easier if radical contrast is the goal: it is always possible to produce letterforms that contrast with the precise forms of type. This exhibition entrance designed by Shin Matsunaga sets the rough edges of drastically enlarged handwriting against smooth typographic letters. Paintings behind the glass wall appear among the letters as decorative fragments. The bright red calligraphy seems to advance and the dark type to recede, thus creating a sense of space appropriate to an architectural composition.

LETTERING AND DESIGN Shin Matsunaga, Tokyo
CLIENT The Seibu Museum of Art, Chiba, Japan

Book Cover

Combining Eastern calligraphy and Western type presents special problems, as the two writing traditions rest on very different formal principles. In order to develop points of harmony and contrast, the formal characteristics of a typeface must be identified, enabling the designer to translate certain elements into the calligraphy. Bodoni, used to set the word 'Opulence', displays unbracketed serifs, sudden transitions from thick to thin elements and vertical weighting. Set as display type, the thin elements recede, leaving a series of nearly separate crescents, bars and triangles in the foreground. Kakuun Matsunaga has used similarly sudden transitions from thick to thin in the calligraphy for this 1983 book cover. As in the Bodoni, the marks that move into the foreground are a series of nearly detached crescents, bars and triangles. But these are very freely written; movement, scale and colour are used as points of contrast.

LETTERING Kakuun
Matsunaga, Tokyo
DESIGN AND ART DIRECTION
Shin Matsunaga, Tokyo
CLIENT Kodansha Ltd

Leaflet Cover
This 1990 piece by Julian Waters uses computer technology to produce a relationship between calligraphic and typographic letters that was not possible before the digital revolution. The design was produced on the Macintosh with Adobe Illustrator. Using the drawing tool, Waters produced two versions of the letters 'AIGA', which appear at the top and bottom of this leaflet cover. The blend option was then used to interpolate eight stages between the calligraphic and typographic versions. With the exception of the final typographic version, printed in black, these were allowed to overlap: the letters 'AIGA' gradually emerge from a nearly solid mass of white marks at the top. On the right is a photograph taken from the computer screen, showing the Bezier points applied to the two drawn versions of the letters in order to create the blend. Producing artwork for such a design by hand would have been enormously time-consuming. In any case, the idea for such a design was only likely to emerge from an understanding of the new potential of digital design.

LETTERING AND DESIGN
Julian Waters, Washington DC
CLIENT AIGA, Washington DC Chapter

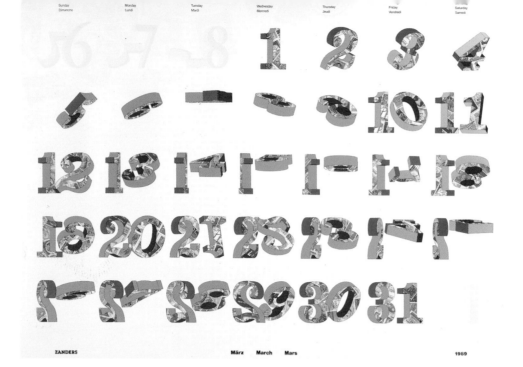

ZANDERS   März   March   Mars   1989

Calendar

The manipulation of type is on occasion a form of game-playing. Igarashi's design of 1989 uses the very basic level of legibility required in calendars as a licence to distort the shapes of the numbers at will. Projected as three-dimensional forms and filled with a collage of international postage stamps, the numbers of the month of March turn somersaults as the weeks pass by.

LETTERING AND DESIGN
Takenobu Igarashi and Noreen Fukumori, Tokyo and Los Angeles
CLIENT Zanders Feinpapiere AG

Interactive Digital Type

Fontworks in London and the international network of Fontshops are pioneering a new approach to type through interactive software. Shown here is F-State, a digital font designed by Neville Brody for the first issue of *Fuse*, Fontworks' forum for the release of experimental postscript typefaces. F-State explores the limits of legibility by creating an interplay of letter shape and counterspace. The font is designed to allow the user to take this exploration further. *Fuse* is seen by its creators as a nebulous realm in which the barriers between type and graphic design dissolve.

DESIGN Neville Brody London
CLIENT *Fuse*

Press Pack
A sense of high-tech urgency emanates from this press pack designed by Why Not Associates for the hair-styling consortium Sebastian. In the centre of the fold-out pack is a photographic image overlaid with a computer-manipulated version of the product logo. The typeface OCR-B is used on the flaps at several different sizes to present legible texts and fragments of words that can only be decoded with effort. The complex shape of this die-cut package is pierced by seemingly meaningful openings. Hairstyling is presented as part of an intelligent and technically precise lifestyle.

LETTERING AND DESIGN
Why Not Associates,
London
CLIENT Sebastian

Exhibition Poster
Manipulated type is used here to illustrate in 1988 the theme of the seventeenth Triennale in Milan. The letters of the words 'Le Città del Mondo e il Futuro delle Metropoli' (World Cities and the future of the Metropolis) were turned into a dense cluster of skyscrapers using the personal computer.

LETTERING AND DESIGN
Italo Lupi, Milan
CLIENT Triennale di Milano

Zufall Spiel

Typographic Experiments
Complex typographic manipulations may be achieved in a few simple steps, and by retaining a sense of play. In 1986 Hans-Rudolf Lutz made several concentric cuts through the words 'Zufall' and 'Spiel' (chance and play). The rings that resulted were then turned by degrees to produce chance configurations of the fragmented letters.

LETTERING Hans-Rudolf Lutz, Zürich

Typographic Experiments
Leonard Currie's piece was produced in 1991 entirely on the photocopier. Dry transfer letters were copied onto clear and coloured films, which were then superimposed and copied again. The textured and layered effects lend a dynamic quality to the composition.

LETTERING AND DESIGN
Leonard Currie, London

Limited Edition Print
Phil Baines used several
simple drawing and printing
techniques to produce this
1987 print. The large
letterforms were drawn
with compass and set-
square and are based on
Anglo-Saxon models; they
were then converted
photographically into zinc
blocks and printed by
letterpress. Gill Sans was
employed to set and
letterpress-print the five
vertical lines of type, and
the large fields of colour
were screen-printed. Thus
the entire piece explores
the relationship of design to
print technology.

LETTERING AND DESIGN
Phil Baines, London

The variety of forms are adapted to the reading requirements of our time. The energetic character of 'San Marco' makes it ideal for extravagant typographical

That's a funny thing about jitterbugs.

They're always above you.

THESE ORIGINAL CHARACTERS, SOMETIMES
NARROW AND SOMETIMES EXPANSIVE,
CREATE A VERY EXPRESSIVE LINE FLOW.
IT IS THEREFORE RECOMMENDED THIS
TYPEFACE BE USED FOR SHORT COPY TEXT.

a a b c d d e e f f g g g g h i j k k
¶ A B C D E F G H I J K L M N O
l m m n nopp p q r r r s s s t t u
P Q R S T U V W X Y Z ❧ Æ Œ
u v v v w w w x x y y y z z z & fi ff

La première Calligraphie Informatique à Ligatures Automatiques

Prix Paris Cité 90 ~ Prix Morisawa 90

François Boltana

The study of historical scripts and of calligraphy are excellent preparations for the design of type. On this page are assembled typefaces by five of the world's leading typographers: Hermann Zapf, Michael Harvey, Adrian Frutiger, Karlgeorg Hoefer and François Boltana. All five men are noted calligraphers who use the understanding of letterforms gained from pen lettering in the design of type. Frutiger's Herculanum, which has been published in the Linotype-Hell 'Type before Gutenberg' series, is based on the informal capitals found in ancient Roman papyrii and inscriptions. The horizontal extension of the 'U' and the 'M' make dramatic breaks in the texture of the line. Entasis and serifs are irregular, giving a spontaneous rhythm to the face.

Michael Harvey's Ellington and Karlgeorg Hoefer's San Marco both return to medieval pen-made prototypes for inspiration. Ellington retains the subtlest hint of its twelfth-century Transitional Gothic origins, while San Marco is frankly based on fifteenth-century Italian Gothic Rotunda.

Hermann Zapf's Renaissance, based on the humanistic scripts of the sixteenth century, provides a wide range of optional characters and special ligatures. These can be used to create breaks in the regular block of text. François Boltana's elegant eighteenth-century copperplate was designed on the Mac and sports a vast number of ligatures and special characters. Here we see typography striving for the variety and fluidity of genuine calligraphy.

Karlgeorg Hoefer:
San Marco
Michael Harvey: Ellington
Adrian Frutiger:
Herculanum
Herman Zapf: Renaissance
François Boltana:
Champion

An eines Olbaums Fuße saß
die Infantin jung und lieblich
Kamm aus Gold in ihren Händen
strich sie pfleglich sich das Haar.
In des Sonnenaufgangs Fächer
ließ sie ihre Blicke schweifen

UND SPRICHT ZU IHM : WAHRLICH/
WAHRLICH/ ICH SAGE EUCH : IHR
WERDET DEN HIMMEL OFFEN SEHEN
UND DIE ENGEL GOTTES HINAUF
UND HERAB FAHREN AUF DES MEN-

Ah mad Arachne! so I saw you there —

already half turned spider — on the shreds

of what you wove to be your own despair.

VERY LARGE SIZES MAY NOT COME

OUT TOO WELL. SERIFS MAY LOOK

TOO THIN, HORIZONTAL BARS MAY

LOOK TOO THICK, OR WHATEVER.

Typefaces occasionally attempt to reproduce the eccentricities and irregularities of hand-made letterforms. In an effort to give printed designs the immediacy of hand-made images, lettering artists are increasingly designing fonts that do not seek to convey the precise regularity expected of type.

Hans-Joachim Burgert has designed several typefaces for his own use that preserve the spontaneity of hand-made marks. Illustrated here are two: Animata and Forma. Both are set on a simple headliner machine for use in the limited-edition books published by Professor Burgert. Animata is a sharp-edged monoline face with unusual arch forms and pronounced tails to the 'g's. Forma is an upper-case font with rough edges and irregular letter heights. Both faces produce rhythmic textures when close-set, and both have been produced using the simplest technology.

Arthur Baker's Visigoth is a photo-comp face originally designed for a fine limited edition of Dante's Divine Comedy, but now generally available. Visigoth is a highly successful typeface that displays traces of both Eastern and Western calligraphy.

Magnus Astrom of Sweden has used Fontographer to convert inscriptional letters designed by Tom Perkins of England into a desktop font. The digitized letterforms retain a good deal of the originality and precision for which Tom Perkins is widely known.

Hans-Joachim Burgert:
Animata
Hans-Joachim Burgert:
Forma
Arthur Baker: Visigoth
Tom Perkins: Inscriptional
letters

Exotic typefaces have an unusual place in the type market. Strange letterforms hold out the promise of novelty and surprise, but if their eccentricities go too far, the forms will quickly become a cliché.

Modern interest in exotic faces can be traced back to the elaborate display faces of the eighteenth and nineteenth centuries. These were used in books and on broadsides, and were occasionally hand-coloured, as in the example shown here. Illustrations, decorative foliage and intricate geometry were all used to produce ornamental letters. These in turn hark back to the illuminated versals of the Middle Ages.

Modern typographers continue to experiment with exotic letterforms. Those shown here are not yet available from type catalogues. Peter Grundy of London designed Circuits in 1982. Though never published, it is well-known in the UK. It makes humorous use of the symbols employed to describe electrical circuitry. Mark Allen of Los Angeles was perhaps inspired by a different kind of wiring to produce the eccentric alphabet shown here. The letterforms resemble doodles, graffiti or maybe the charts used by football coaches to describe elaborate playing-field strategies.

F- Newida (left, designed by Erik van Blokland) and F-Flixel (designed by Just van Rossum) demonstrate a new approach to digital type design. Commissioned for *Fuse* magazine, they attempt to establish new parameters of legibility that take into account our intuitive faculties.

Victorian block book
Peter Grundy: Alphabet of circuits
Mark Allen: Alphabet
Erik van Blokland: F-Newida
Just van Rossum: F-Flixel

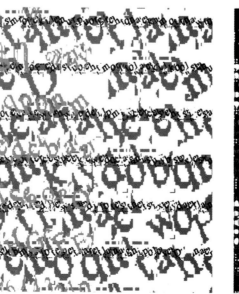

Man and nature produce new letterforms by happy accident every day: the designer need only open his eyes to discover a limitless supply of strange and wonderful letters in rocks, trees, tools, refuse.... Presented here are three examples of alphabets produced in unconventional ways. Joyce Cutler Shaw's alphabet translates the twenty-six letters of the Latin alphabet into configurations of bird bones. The reader must identify very subtle differences in the arrangements of bones to read the text. Subtleties of this kind are alien to Western readers accustomed to the simple forms of the Latin alphabet. But to a Chinese or a Japanese reader, such fine distinctions are the norm.

Mervyn Kurlansky of Pentagram has also explored legibility in his alphabet of studio objects, many of which are easily recognized as letters. Others, such as the wall-plug 'f' and the key-ring 'q' could only be seen as letterforms in a particular context. Once the game is begun, however, letterforms will spring up all over the studio.

Medieval scribes often forced standing or sitting figures into the shapes of letters. In the eighteenth century, silhouettes of peasants and gentry gracefully delineated the twenty-six letters. Victorian display faces often relied on grotesque distortions of the human form to produce alphabets. In the poster by Toshiyasu Nanbu, elegant hand gestures are used to spell out the word 'PEACE'. The gestures are serene and natural. At the centre, the letter 'A' is composed of hands in prayer.

Joyce Cutler Shaw: Bird bone alphabet
Mervyn Kerlansky/Pentagram: Studio objects
Toshiyasu Nanbu: Alphabet of hands

1945年8月6日午前8時15分, 広島市は閃光に包まれた。

Experimental Lettering
A Minolta black-and-white
copier was used to manipulate dry transfers letters in
this recent experimental
piece by Leonard Currie.
The first A3 copy was put
back through the machine
eight times. Each time, the
image on the glass was
moved, enlarged, reduced
or changed altogether.

LETTERING AND DESIGN
Leonard Currie, London

The Design of Letters

Hand-lettering and type play very different roles in graphic design. The simple geometry and even textures of type ensure legibility in any context. But these very qualities limit the visual impact of unmanipulated type. Hand-lettering, by contrast, achieves maximum visual impact by altering the simple geometry and even textures of type. Legibility is ensured by the context and by the unique identity of hand-made letters.

This chapter will explore the formal principles on which hand-lettering is based. These principles are closer to those of the fine arts than to the theories that govern the design of type. The regular shapes and spaces of type give way to more dramatic themes and variations. The consistent textures of type are replaced in hand-lettering by contrasts of light and dark, thick and thin, large and small. Though the lettering artist must understand typographic conventions in order to produce legible letters, he or she does not merely enliven typographic forms. All those who work with letters must build up compositions of form, line and colour with the appropriate emotional content.

Although a great deal has been written on the principles of composition and colour in relation to the fine arts, nothing has yet been published that applies these same theories to the design of letters. Hans-Joachim Burgert's study *The Calligraphic Line,* which exists in typescript only, is the most important effort yet to be made to produce a theoretical foundation for the subject. Burgert stresses that the primary tool of the calligrapher (and by extension to all who work with letters) is the line. In a composition of letters, he states, 'primary and secondary themes must be chosen. Certain forms are emphasized within the structure of the composition without compromising the principles of the alphabet. A calligraphic composition has its own inner logic, which accompanies the verbal content of the work while retaining its independence.' For example, in a composition of letters, the shapes of the letters may be reduced to triangles, rectangles and circles. These are the themes. Certain of these geometric forms must be made larger than the others to serve as focal points. The spaces between and within the shapes also need to be varied in relations to the overall composition. Colours and textures can play a vital role in establishing these relationships.

f in our work we find these
things: personal satisfaction;
contribution in a spirit of service;
a sense of community; reward
and recognition—there is value
beyond things to treasure . . .

CMP

Catalogue
Jean Evans used a broad
pen with a right-oblique
edge to write these
energetic italic letters for
the cover of this 1986
catalogue. This tool
produced the wedge-like
ends of the main strokes
and made it possible to give
an extreme slope to the
letters without losing the
counter-spaces. The
calligraphy was reversed
out and given a spectral tint
from orange to yellow. It
was then overprinted with a
special varnish, causing it to
shine brilliantly from the
matt black background.

LETTERING
Jean Evans, Boston
DESIGN AND ART DIRECTION
Bob Paganucci, Boston
CLIENT Nynex

As the work in this book shows, the formal themes used to build up compositions of letters can come from any source: nature (a lattice of branches, the veining in stones); technology (industrial forms, crude machine-made letters); history (ancient manuscripts, Victorian shopfronts); works of art (Cubist paintings, Chinese porcelains); and found objects (refuse, graffiti, chance configurations of objects, studio tools).

Owing to the requirements of legibility that will guide the making of most letters for graphic design, it is rarely possible to take the completely free approach advocated by Hans-Joachim Burgert. Nor can the strict geometry and even textures of typography produce sufficiently dramatic shapes for most purposes. The graphic designer's territory is somewhere between these two extremes. He or she must achieve a judicious blend of form and function. The best way to show how this can be done is to examine several examples of hand-lettering and to analyse the formal themes that make up the whole composition of letterforms. Calligraphic letters, geometric letters and computer-generated letters will be examined in turn.

The calligraphy produced by Jean Evans of Boston for the Nynex Service Recognition Program catalogue has all the freedom and life of the best calligraphy of any age. The main brochure has six calligraphic titles, the one represented here occurring on the title page. This same title design is blind-embossed and varnished on the cover. Jean Evans has used a broad pen to produce strokes that vary in thickness from the almost closed form of the 'a' in 'Program' to the fine hairlines of the 'o' in the same word. The letterforms are basically italic, crossbred with the casual forms of handwriting. Owing to the oblique cut of the pen's edge, most straight strokes have chiselled terminals rather than hook serifs. These sloped terminals lean into the direction of reading. The words rush forward at great speed, lending a dynamic corporate image to Nynex. The shapes and spaces that make up the words are tightly packed; only the capitals and descenders break out of the solid group. Thus the letters, though lively, are regularly spaced, and entirely appropriate to a piece of corporate literature.

Architectural Lettering
Architectural lettering makes particular demands on the designer, successfully solved by David Harris in his painted inscription of 1984 for Exeter College of Art and Design. The mural occupies a cement-rendered wall nearly forty feet wide. The scale drawing was transferred by snapping the straight lines with chalked string and swinging the circular lines with a simple 'compass' of chalk on the end of a string. The painting was done in Sikken emulsions over two weeks. These show little sign of weathering after several years, and highlight the fact that hand-lettering can have an important contribution to make to the aesthetic quality of public spaces.

LETTERING AND DESIGN
David Harris, Exeter
CLIENT Exeter College of Art and Design

Letters conceived as geometric forms are occasionally used to produce abstract compositions. The façade of Exeter College of Art and Design, designed by David Harris, shows letters that have been reduced to basic geometric concepts in order to relate them to their architectural setting. The painted inscription occupies a flat projecting wall above the entrance to the college. The façade of the building, which lacks architectural distinction, consists of horizontal bands of large windows separated by pan tiles. Wide aluminium mullions divide the stripes of glass into smaller rectangular segments. The building has the grid-like arrangement characteristic of much modern architecture.

These basic concepts have been taken over by David Harris as the structure of his inscription. The surface is divided into three horizontal bands that correspond to specific features of the facade. The letters take the form of linear and geometric shapes which are integrated by modifying the relationship of figure to ground. In the central band the counter-shapes of the linear letters come forward and the letters themselves recede. In the upper and lower bands this relationship is reversed: most of the linear letterforms come forward as light figures on a dark ground. The first letters of the words 'Art' and 'Design' are enlarged to form a kind of logo that moves across the three bands and ties them together. David Harris has thus given considerable aesthetic interest to a mediocre facade that at the same time can serve as an identity for the college.

The design of letters on the computer presents special problems to the lettering artist. Unlike such tools as pencils, brushes and chisels, the mouse is incapable of providing variable tactile sensations. It can, of course, be moved more or less swiftly, producing marks of a different quality. But that quality is never 'understood' by the hand as a physical sensation. Textures, layers and all other manipulations of the surface of the page must be brought in as intellectual decisions.

The work of April Greiman in Los Angeles frequently relies on computer-generated letterforms. Reproduced here is a poster designed in 1985 which combines a variety of digital and hand techniques to produce a layered image. 'Sequences' is a brand of textured papers produced by the Simpson Paper Company. The

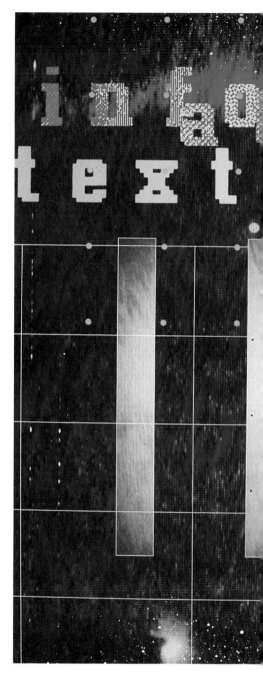

Advertisement for a Paper Company
The transition from photo-typesetting to computer-generated letters presents certain challenges. The letterforms of the film age were inherited from the age of lead. Both of these technologies allowed continuous curves and exceptionally sharp definition. Digital technology reduces all letterforms to a bitmap, and curves can only be represented by step patterns; the smaller the step pattern, the sharper the definition of the curve. But it takes very high-resolution printers to compete with the sharpness of photo-typesetting, and these are not available to every desktop publisher. Thus a few designers are asking if the typefaces of the film age can serve the needs of the digital age. This 1985 piece by April Greiman represents a possible solution to the problem.

LETTERING AND DESIGN April Greiman, Los Angeles VIDEOGRAPHY April Greiman, Los Angeles CLIENT Simpson Paper Company background texture of the poster designed to advertise this product was created by filming a piece of cloth at very close range with a video camera attached by modem to an Apple Mac. This video image was then coloured and manipulated into a series of overlapping planes using MacPaint. The grid of white lines and orange dots was produced using the drawing tool in the same program.

The words 'information' and 'texture' were set in April Greiman's own digital typeface 'Monaco' and further manipulated on the Mac for this design. Standard Mac textures were applied to some letters, while others were given graduated tints. The word 'information' was split and overlapped. Finally, paint splatters were scanned in and included in the artwork. Film for four-colour printing could then be made directly from the computer.

The operations just described (with the exception of film-making) are all possible in a studio possessing a Mac linked by modem to a video camera. Here they have been used to produce a multi-layered image with vibrant colours and intricate texture. The letterforms are fully integrated into the image. They overlap and recede in space like the planes of texture and colour. Their bitmap quality is in harmony with the grid on which the whole design is placed. As with the experimental typefaces of Neville Brody and Jon Wozencroft discussed in the final chapter, these frankly digital forms demonstrate a desire to design typefaces appropriate to the new technology.

The three examples of tailor-made lettering considered above show successful responses to specific design problems. In each case the letterforms were designed to take full advantage of particular materials and techniques. Over the next few pages a wide range of techniques for producing and manipulating letters is presented. The examples have been chosen for their ability to represent the potential of particular tools and materials. Craftsmanship in lettering means using the chosen technology, whether calligraphic pen or Macintosh computer, to the full. Both lettering artist and graphic designer must develop an understanding of the formal potential of their particular tools and materials in order to produce confident and effective letterforms.

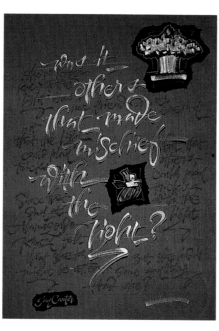

Pen-made Letters

The simpler the mark-making tool, the more versatile it is. Pens, pencils, charcoal and crayons will never be exhausted as sources of new and exciting letterforms. Shown here is calligraphy written with a quill pen by the author for the film *Prospero's Books*. The goose quill is ideal for producing inky historical letters, such as these; but it can also make sharp, refined and very modern forms. Other simple mark-making tools include ruling pens, scrapers on scraper board, felt tips, ball point pens, and fountain pens. The character of the mark depends on the tool, ink and writing surface. Rough-edged letters are made easily on textured water colour paper. Balsa wood dipped in watery ink will produce dragged marks with a puddled ink effect. Experimentation is essential to discover the limitless potential of these simple tools.

Brush-made Letters

Brushes are equally versatile mark-making tools. The blue letters shown here were painted by Carl Rohrs of Los Angeles using a broad edged brush and thick poster paints on textured paper. Thinner paint would have reduced the 'dragged' look of the letters and resulted in sharper edges. Brushes come in hundreds of shapes and sizes, from fine sable brushes that taper to a point, to Chinese brushes, house painting brushes and even rough bristled plastic brushes. Controlling a brush takes some skill, and practice is needed before elegant letters such as these can be made confidently. But more casual and even eccentric letters are a natural product of experimentation with brushes. As with pens, the type of ink or paint used, as well as the surface, crucially affects the style and quality of the final product.

Drawn Letters

Drawing and writing are slightly different processes. Written letters reveal the rhythmic movements of the hand and the tactile qualities of the tools and materials used to make them. Drawn letters are generally more deliberate and controlled, being built up more slowly of several strokes. These letters were drawn by Julian Waters of Washington D.C. The forms were then inked and slightly retouched for reproduction. The distribution of weight, especially in curved strokes, will differ between drawn letters and those written with a broad-edged pen. Both techniques require skill, in particular to create serifed Roman capitals. But a profound understanding of the complex shapes of these letters is needed to draw them with a pointed tool.

Film Cutting

Film cutting is an important source of precise and sharp edged letterforms. These letters by Freda Sack of London were cut from two colours of rubylith film using a hand-held blade. The sharp edges ensured by confident movements of the knife through film made this technique ideal for producing final artwork for photocomp typefaces. In the digital age the technique is still useful for producing logos and other one-off letterforms, as well as artwork for photolithography. An experimental approach to the use of rubylith films might include tearing, photocopying, layering, crumpling, and so on. A related area is stencil cutting. Stencils can be used to trace down, paint or spray letters on virtually any surface. Stencilled letters are generally much rougher than film-cut letters, and thus communicate a greater spontaneity.

Collage

These letters by Crescent Lodge of London were made by pasting torn fragments of newspapers into the forms of enlarged typographic letters. The collage technique is very flexible and allows almost anything to be transformed into a letter: newspaper and magazine clippings, bits of foil and tissue, cloth, plastic and even glass. Collage has been used by many artists in the twentieth century, including Pablo Picasso, Kurt Schwitters and Jasper Johns, to incorporate letterforms and whole texts into their paintings.

Hand-manipulated Type

More drastic transformations of typographic letters are also possible. To produce this design for a record jacket, Rob O'Connor of Stylorouge in London enlarged a composition of dry-transfer letters on the photocopier, crunched the enlargement up with his hands, spread it out again, and recopied it - a few simple steps to create unique hand-lettering. Stylorouge rejoice in such basic manipulations of type. They have wrapped dry transfer letters around tubes to produce curved shapes, and they have photocopied letters through superimposed tints to produce a moirée effect. The simpler the approach, the more variations are possible.

Wire Letters

Happy Massee of New York created these wire letters as a title for a magazine article on wire furniture. Wire, tin, plastic and a wide range of other materials can be cut and shaped with scissors and pliers. Plastic-coated electrical wire comes in many colours and widths. Tin and plastic can be bought as sheets or cut from cans and cartons. Automotive suppliers often carry an assortment of self-adhesive plastic sheets with metallic and holographic finishes, from which letters can be cut. Such materials are often used to produce the modern urban equivalent of folk art.

Cloth Letters

Christine Büttner of London designed this television prop, which was executed in appliqué using shot silk and black glass beads. The silk banner was waved in front of the television camera like a matador's cape and served to separate the titles and credits of a television identity sequence. Embroidery, appliqué and needlepoint have been used for centuries to produce letterforms. The fashion industry relies heavily on machine embroidered letterforms on sweatshirts and t-shirts. These same forms and techniques are available to the graphic designer. Other cloth-working techniques include screen-printing, painting and dyeing. Each fabric has its own characteristics and responds to the paints and dyes in a different way. The modern textile industry has produced an astonishing array of new fibres that could inspire the designer.

Letter Cut in Brick

One of Britain's leading lettercutters, Richard Kindersley, cut this R in brick as a trial for a large architectural inscription. Lettering artists such as Kindersley have pioneered a whole range of new inscriptional styles and techniques. These are of special interest to architects and the designers of retail outlets. Slate, marble, limestone, granite, wood and even man-made materials are suitable for chisel-cut letters. These need not remain in architectural settings, but can be included as photographic images in designs for print.

Found Letters

Letters do not always have to be made. They can also be found in nature, on the street and in discarded objects. Found letters and letters discovered in familiar objects are featured throughout this book. Mervyn Kurlansky of Pentagram in London discovered an entire alphabet in the tools of his design studio. Other lettering artists have found alphabets in the veining of river pebbles, in crushed beer cans and in configurations of branches. Ploughing patterns photographed from the air have yielded alphabets, as have the fibres embedded in the surface of hand-made paper. Finally, of course, there is history: manuscripts, works of art, pottery and textiles from almost every century and culture contain unique letterforms. These can be used straight from the source or transformed by hand or on the computer to produce new shapes.

Letter Painted on Glass

Victorian and Edwardian sign-writers created exuberant letterforms on glass using paint, acid etching and gold leaf. The styles developed by these early lettering artists have continued in use to the present day. Carl Rohrs of Los Angeles has taken this lively tradition further by applying new materials such as opalescent paints and thin sheets of genuine mother-of-pearl to the surface of the glass. As with letters cut in stone and wood, this work is of particular relevance to architects and the designers of shops and restaurants. But the same forms can be included in artwork for print where special print finishing techniques such as varnishes, foil stamping and embossing can heighten the Victorian splendour of the letters.

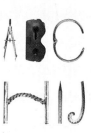

Typewritten Letters
Lettering can be created and manipulated on many of the machines present in most design studios. The letterforms produced by typewriters can suggest the immediacy of journalism, for example. By typing and overtyping, complex images of letterforms are possible. This image created by Joan Dobkin of Bloomfield Hills, Michigan for Amnesty International uses typewritten letters to convey a sense of reportage. Extreme enlargements of typewritten letters reveal their rough edges, adding a sense of urgency. Typographic errors, dropped letters and manual corrections suggest a human presence largely absent from text type.

Letters Manipulated by Fax
These letterforms were distorted by using the copy option on an Amstrad fax machine. By gently slowing and turning the original while it passed through the machine, the letters were twisted and stretched, producing a three-dimensional effect. This process was done as an experiment only and is almost certainly not a use of the machine that would be recommended by the manufacturers.

Letters Manipulated by Fax
Paul Elliman has used the fax machine and photocopier to produce this monumental image of generic beer cans. The enlarged image occupied several A4 sheets, which were connected to form long strips. These strips were then faxed to a small circle of friends, who were required to reassemble the image.

Letters Manipulated by Photocopier
Leonard Currie of London has used the photocopier to stretch and distort typographic letters in this experimental piece. By moving the image on the glass while the copy is being made, the letters were stretched and twisted. This image was then further distorted by movement, enlargement and reduction over several generations of photocopying. By copying one manipulated image onto another, textures are built up. These can serve as background to legible type. Typographic images can also be spun, crunched and torn while the copy is being made.

Letters Manipulated by Photocopier
A Canon colour copier was used by Leonard Currie to create this image. Colour copiers scan an image three times to separate out and print yellow, cyan and magenta. Black is created by overlapping these three colours. This piece began as black and white artwork, which was moved on the glass after each scan, thus separating and partially overlapping the primary colours. Where the primary colours overlapped secondary colours were produced. This process was repeated with the new colour copy on the glass, and so on for several generations. Finally, the copier's plotting stylus was used to isolate large rectangles of yellow and magenta on the image.

Omnichrom Letters
Omnichrom films are generally used to produce colour mock-ups for presentations to clients. As this experimental piece by Leonard Currie shows, omnichrom has other uses as well. If a photocopy is made with no artwork on the glass and the cover open, a completely black sheet results. A used omnichrom sheet (ie with lettering already 'pulled out' of the solid colour) can then be applied to this black photocopy to produce black letters on a coloured ground. By using a hand-held heat source further omnichrom colours can be applied to specific areas of the image, which can be rephotocopied and re-coloured over several generations to produce complex textures such as this.

Cast Cement Letters

These cast cement letters by Richard Kindersley of London were conceived as sculptural ornaments for a landscape garden. Though most graphic design studios are not equipped to produce letters in cast cement, the technique is fairly simple and can be attempted, on a smaller scale then represented here of course, by anyone with basic do-it-yourself skills. Another cement technique, reverse casting, is especially useful for creating lettering on cast cement facades. This is normally done by cutting the letterforms out of plywood and applying them to the inside face of the casting form. When the cement has been cast and has set, the form is removed, leaving the letters as negative shapes in the cement surface.

Perspex Letter

This 'T' was cut and assembled in perspex by the Tokyo-based lettering artist Takenobu Igarashi. Igarashi is known for the impeccable technical precision of his sculptural pieces, which bring letterforms into the world of high-tech engineering. Plastic and perspex are, of course, the most common supports for letters on shop fascias and in public signage. The general standard of design in these spheres is usually low. But Igarashi's piece reveals the aesthetic potential of these inexpensive materials.

Metal Letter

Takenobu Igarashi has used steel, bronze, aluminium and other metals to produce sculptural letterforms displaying perfect craftsmanship. Such pieces can only be created using industrial lathes, drill presses and polishers. Metal can also be used to create rough, crude and aggressive letterforms, however. Sheet steel, corrugated iron, scrap metal and even engine parts can be cut, and welded to produce architectural lettering and lettering for inclusion as photographic images in designs for print.

Letters
Sand-blasted in Glass

Pieter Boudens of Bruges combined inscriptional letters in stone with letters sand-blasted in glass in this piece. Sand-blasting, acid etching, screen printing and engraving can all be used to produce lettering on glass. These techniques, which require specialist knowledge, are frequently used to produce lettering for architectural applications. Here Boudens has achieved a unique effect by placing lettering on a transparent plane over lettering on a solid plane.

Film-cut Letters

The letters on this glass wall announce an exhibition by the Japanese artist Damoto. They were designed by Shin Matsunaga of Tokyo and cut from self-adhesive film using a computer-guided stencil cutter. This technique allows letters to be produced on a monumental scale by dividing them into sections with the help of the computer and cutting them from film section by section with the stencil cutter.

Airbrushed Letters

Airbrushes have been used for decades to produce lettering for commercial design. In this piece, Koichi Sato of Tokyo has used an airbrush to give a halo to his own Japanese brush calligraphy. This is a modern application of a technique generally used for art deco and other 'nostalgic' styles. Airbrush artists are also called upon to imitate street styles such as graffiti. Metallic, marbled and translucent effects are also possible with an airbrush.

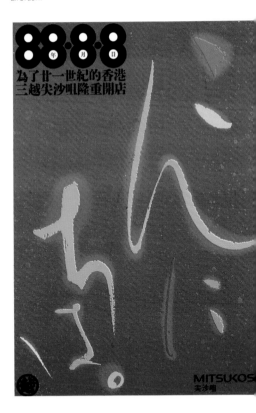

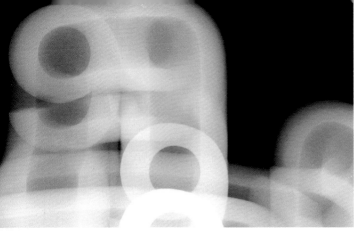

Number Moved Before Camera

A hand-held camera set to a slow shutter speed was used to capture the moving number 9 seen in this image. Leonard Currie simply cut the number from white card and moved it in front of a black background while the photograph was being made. In some places the number can still be recognized. In others it becomes a blur of lines resembling neon.

Letters Projected on a Model

Leonard Currie began this piece by making a sculpture of cut card resembling a maze or an architectural model. A 35mm transparency of type was then projected onto the model using a slide projector. Owing to the way the light struck the variously tilted planes, different shadows and distortions of the letterforms were created.

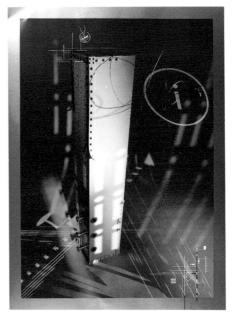

Constructed Letters

This elaborate model was constructed by Alan Kemp following designs produced by Liz Friedman for the BBC in London and filmed with a 35mm tracking camera. Beginning at 'ground' level, where the model resembles groups of architectural ruins, the camera moved upwards until the ruins could be seen to spell out the work "Chronicle". The model itself is highly detailed and required several days to align for shooting. Such a piece could only be produced on a generous budget and with the most up-to-date technology.

Constructed Letter

This letter 'I' forms a part of a three-dimensional model of the word 'Smirnoff' constructed by Why Not Associates of London. A slide projector was used to cast a computer-generated image in white light across the model. The little toy helicopter was added during the shoot on an impulse and is said to bear no relation to the other elements of the composition. The whole set was then photographed for print.

Neon Lettering

April Greiman designed this identity for the China Club, a popular Los Angeles restaurant. The logo was executed in neon and applied to the restaurant's façade and interior. Architectural neon can include moving parts and sequences of flashing letters. It is now being combined with letters in other media such as polished steel and back-lit plastic. The use of neon is not restricted to architectural applications. It is often included in designs for print as well.

Back-lit Characters

This poster by Shin Matsunaga of Tokyo appears to be either neon or computer-generated. In fact is was created by a much simpler process. The Japanese characters were first cut out of black paper, the openings covered with coloured acetate and back-lit. Finally, the piece was photographed with a slow shutter speed, allowing the coloured light to blur.

Mechanised Letters

Margaret Horrocks and Jane Wyatt of the BBC in London designed these festive three-dimensional letters with moving parts to serve as a Christmas identity sequence. A small motor moved the cross bar of the 'T' and the sweets on the top of the 'W' up and down; the 'O' started to spin; and the arms of the 'W' moved in and out, creating a child-like fantasy of movement and colour.

Cast-light Letters

A 35mm transparency was used by Art Chantry of Seattle to cast type across a male torso in this theatre poster. The word wraps around the body and distorts the letters. The image clearly refers to police line-ups and conveys a hard, sinister feeling.

Illuminated Plastic Letters

The model constructed for this album cover included letters cut from heavy clear plastic. Placed around a planet on Saturn-like rings, the back-lit letters make nostalgic reference to 1920s and 30s diners. The techniques for creating such letterforms are the special domain of the signage industry. Materials such as light refracting plastics and optical fibres are increasingly used for commercial signage. These materials also present new opportunities to the graphic designer and lettering artist.

Back-lit Steel Letters

This back-lit sign of cut steel sheeting was designed by Toshiyasu Nanbu of Tokyo. The patina of the steel is the result of torch cutting and rusting. Metals such as steel, copper, bronze and aluminium can be chemically patinated to produce a wide range of colours and textures. Unprotected metals will gradually develop rich patinas through exposure to the elements.

Foil-blocked Letters

Foil blocking has long been used to suggest dazzling extravagance. This alphabet by Julian Waters was blocked with a holographic foil. Foils now come in an enormous range of finishes, including marbled, brushed, opalescent and multi-coloured metallic foils. As with embossing, foil blocking is usually available only from a print-finisher.

Die-cut Letters

The letterforms in this card designed by Italo Lupi of Milan were cut with specially made metal dies. When unfolded, the openings spell out the word 'AUGURI'. When folded, the overlapping windows produce an abstract design of coloured shapes. This piece is a fine example of an area that is increasingly being explored by graphic designers: card and book structures. Die cutting is particularly useful for making fold-out and pop-up structures.

Screen-printed Letters

Screen printing is frequently used to achieve intense colours and bright metallic effects on large scale designs for print. This poster by Lorenzo Homar of Puerto Rico was hand printed in four colours. Though expert screen printers can maintain sharpness on even fairly small letterforms, the medium does not allow the reproduction of letters eight point and smaller without loss of detail. But it does give far more solid and vibrant colours than offset lithography. Special colours and coatings now available for screen process printing include opalescent, dayglow and glitter inks.

Hand-printed Letters

Hans Schmidt of Baden Hard in Germany has used simple wooden blocks to hand-print this poster in green and red. Subtle textures and colour gradations were produced by overlapping the stamped colours in some areas and using strongly grained blocks in others. Virtually any flat surface can be used as a printing block, including card, linoleum, rubber erasers, rubber rollers and even cut potatoes. Old wooden display type can also be inked and pressed onto paper by hand. Such monoprints can then be incorporated into designs for photo-lithography.

Letterpress Letters

These letters were printed onto corrugated cardboard by letterpress. Planungsteam K Nengelken of Cologne used wooden display types inked by hand to impress the letters deeply into the undulating surface of the cardboard. The ink was squeezed out in some places and failed to make contact in others, thus producing rough, broken and crude letterforms. In earlier times letterpress printing was used to achieve a sharpness and blackness that offset printing still cannot match. Today it is often used on letterheads and business cards to suggest quality and care, but here the usual significance of the technique is inverted.

136

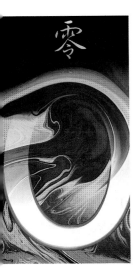

Computer-integrated Letter

For this poster Mitsuo Katsui of Tokyo used the Response programme to integrate a typographic letter 'O' with a photograph of the patterns made by oil floating on water. The colours of the original photograph (which was scanned in using a high resolution colour scanner) were digitally enhanced to produce the psychedelic effect. The image was then colour-separated and prepared for print. Before committing resources for plate-making, it is now possible at certain copy centres to print out a full colour digital design straight from the disc.

Computer-generated Letters

The Apple Mac was used by April Greiman of Los Angeles to give a grid-like quality to all the elements of this poster. The background texture, produced by importing a close-up video image of a textile, is echoed in the stepped silhouettes of the digitally designed letterforms. Many of the letters are filled with standard Mac textures, while others were given graduated tints. Film for four-colour printing was made directly from the disc.

Computer-blended Letters

Julian Waters fused calligraphic and drawn letters in this design by using the blend option of the Adobe Fontographer programme. The hand-written and hand-drawn letters were scanned in and marked with Bezier points. Each point on a calligraphic letter was paired with another on the corresponding drawn letter. The number of blend steps was then chosen and the blend option applied.

Computer-manipulated Letters

These spinning typographic numbers are taken from a calendar designed by Takenobu Igarashi of Tokyo. The marbled paper pattern was scanned in and applied to the front face of the numbers. All remaining manipulations including the shading, spinning and three-dimensional modelling of the numbers, are computer-generated.

Digital Type Design

Tom Perkins of Cambridgeshire and Magnus Åstrôm of Umeå in Sweden collaborated in the production of this digital typeface. The original drawings were done by Perkins in pencil on paper. These were scanned into an Apple Mac using a 300 dpi scanner. The linear forms were then plotted with Bezier points using Fontographer software. The digitalized alphabet was then used to generate light, bold and outline fonts. Each font was digitally adjusted where necessary to produce harmonious forms and consistent spacing.

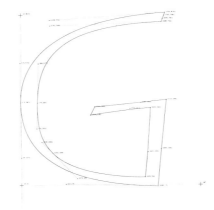

Computer-generated Number

Jacqueline Casey and David Small of the Visible Language Workshop in Cambridge, Massachusetts, produced this postcard to celebrate the fifth anniversary of the MIT Media Lab. The image was created using watercolour simulation software developed by David Small for the Connection Machine. Many software packages are now coming on the market that use highly complex digital technology to simulate basic hand techniques. With such programmes the world of hand-lettering has come full circle to end where it began thousands of years ago.

137

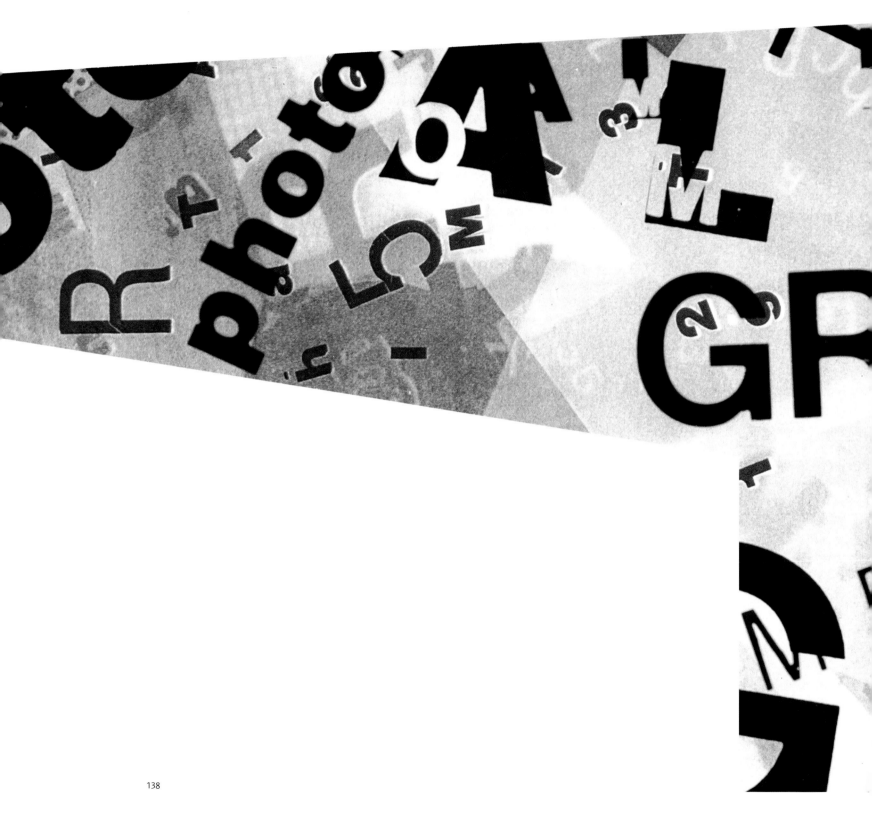

Experimental Lettering
Leonard Currie used dry
transfer lettering and a
Minolta black and white
copier to create this
experimental piece. The
first photocopy was fed
through the machine ten
times, and each time the
image on the glass was
enlarged, reduced, moved
or changed altogether.
Finally, the original artwork
and the last generation
were both made into 35mm
slides, which were mounted
together in one slide frame.
When shot for reproduction
in this book, the upper layer
of glass in this double slide
was unavoidably out of
focus.

LETTERING AND DESIGN
Leonard Currie, London

New Directions

The computer is having a considerable impact on the use of hand-lettering for graphic design. To identify new trends in the designing of letters, it is therefore important to ask what the effects of the digital revolution are likely to be; for it is generally recognized that all aspects of graphic design will be so transformed in the next few years by the introduction of design-related software that the industry will barely resemble its present self. Indeed according to some observers it is not only graphic design that will be transformed. The British film director Peter Greenaway, referring to his film *Prospero's Books*, has said, 'The Paintbox, as its name suggests, links the vocabulary of electronic picture-making to the traditions of the artist's pen, palette and brush, with the same essential ability to permit a personal signature. I believe its possibilities will radically alter cinema, television, photography, painting and printing (and maybe much else) to degrees of sophistication never before considered.'

With the whole of our visual and even literary and musical culture under such pressure from a single machine, there is understandable concern on the part of those graphic designers who have yet to master (or even acquire access to) the new technology that they may be losing a design race. Other designers actually avoid computer graphics altogether for fear of becoming mechanistic keyboard operators. It would seem that a chasm is opening up between high- and low-tech designers.

Or is there? Will the personal computer really destroy the last remaining manual skills of the graphic designer (calligraphy, drawing, paste-up...)? Will MacTaste shove aside all the other high- and low-tech styles that jostle with each other on the pages of this book? Do styles change only because the technology changes?

Surely it is not as simple as that. Most of the designers approached during the compilation of this book have stressed that the personal computer has proved a useful addition to the long list of tools and techniques used to originate and manipulate letterforms. My own experiences as the calligrapher for *Prospero's Books* indicate that the Paintbox makes it possible to integrate the works of countless artists operating in various media into one larger and supremely sophisticated work of art. Indeed, the computer is above all an integrator. It therefore encourages rather than discourages the further development of manual skills.

141

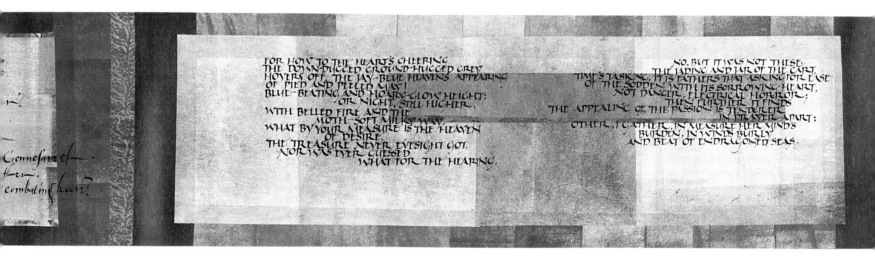

Experimental Calligraphy

Illustrated here is part of one out of six eight-foot-long scrolls, produced in 1991, containing verses of Gerard Manley Hopkins' poem *The Wreck of the Deutschland*. In order to produce this piece, a new technique for colouring and collaging Chinese tissue was developed using water-based lino inks applied with rubber rollers. Traditional Chinese scroll-mounting methods were subtly modified to paste the pieces of coloured tissue together, and the completed scroll was sized and burnished to prepare it for writing. The calligraphy was written with a quill with a minimum of planning, and hence with a considerable element of risk.

LETTERING AND DESIGN
Brody Neuenschwander,
Bruges, Belgium

And the computer aesthetic? The first generation of computer graphics has been characterized by a dazzling visual and linguistic complexity. So dominant has its style been that many designers have used the older technology to imitate it. But just as the excesses of the Baroque and Rococo were followed by the refined simplicity of Neo-Classicism, so too a new simplicity and classicism promises to succeed the initial elaborate style.

Classic proportions, compositions and letterforms never disappear for long. What does change permanently is human perception and thought, and here it is that developments of real interest are taking place. As so often in the past it is the fine rather than the applied arts that lead the way in developing new forms of expression.

In both typography and calligraphy, remarkable work is being done. Following developments in twentieth-century painting, calligraphers such as Hans-Joachim Burgert, who has a private press in Berlin, are applying principles of abstract composition to Western letterforms. For although Burgert claims that the invention of printing in the fifteenth century relieved calligraphy of the burden of providing legible texts and freed it to become a true art form, it was not until the development of abstraction in painting and sculpture in the twentieth century that similar developments in calligraphy were made. The result has been a true flowering of lettering as art in the West: witness for example the calligraphic marks of the American calligrapher and typographer Arthur Baker, which refer to the tradition of illusionism in Western painting by playing on the idea of sculptural form. The abstract and three-dimensional potential of the Latin alphabet has also been realized by artists such as Hans Schmidt and Takenobu Igarashi.

Similar developments are taking place in typography. *Fuse,* the British avant-garde type magazine and software package of Neville Brody and Jon Wozencroft, for example, is exploring aspects of legibility that may in time be applicable to commercial design. Wozencroft is attempting to encourage the design of letterforms that are entirely appropriate to digital technology and at the same time force the reader intuitively to decode the messages they carry.

Hans Rudolf Lutz in Zürich and Joyce Cutler Shaw in California are exploring other aspects of codes and language systems. Both

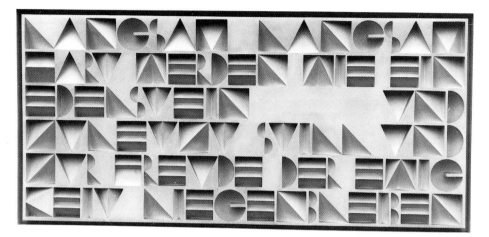

Poetic Inscription

Many of this century's most fascinating developments in the field of lettering have taken place in the German-speaking world. Hans Schmidt is one of the few modern lettering artists to achieve widespread recognition outside the field of lettering and typography. This moulded plastic inscription, undertaken in 1970, displays the penetration to essentials of form and meaning characteristic of Hans Schmidt's work. The text, taken from Nietzsche, reads: 'Slowly, slowly become hard like a jewel... and come to rest in peace and eternal joy'. Schmidt has used a literal representation of these words by converting the letterforms into the facets of a cut diamond; light and shadow play over the surface as they would over a brilliant stone. Letterforms are thus brought into the third dimension without sacrificing their graphic power.

LETTERING AND DESIGN
Hans Schmidt, Baden Hard, Germany

Woodblock Print

Hans Schmidt has made many attempts to capture the singular power of the words 'Ich bin' (I am). Spoken by Yahweh to Moses, the words resonate with the existential truth and finality of the Jewish faith. This 1979 wood-block print explores this statement of being by reducing the letters to their final and absolute identity. They are legible, but only in this context; they are self-referential. It is impossible to conceive of the complete alphabet reduced to such a minimalist statement. Only here, only these shapes and words can carry the message.

LETTERING AND DESIGN
Hans Schmidt, Baden Hard, Germany

144

formulate alphabets that break down barriers between different cultures. Lutz has attempted to identify the 'hieroglyphics of today' in the symbols applied to sealed crates to indicate contents and methods of handling; Shaw has constructed an alphabet of anatomically correct bird bones in which individual letters can be recognized only by observing differences of a very subtle kind. To read the bird bones requires powers of observation more in keeping with Chinese and Japanese than with Western habits of reading.

The London-based artist and typographer Paul Elliman has developed the concept of 'Wild Typography', which attempts to recapture the medium of typography for the common man. In Elliman's view, industry and a rather esoteric design world have taken control of the main medium of communication - type - for purely commercial purposes. Elliman feels that most people are alienated from type, and that its expressive potential must be made accessible to all through education in order to change the way the alphabet is used in society. Elliman explores the nature of language and the arbitrary system of the alphabet in his conceptual magazine Box Space (page 148). Elliman describes his publication as the 'overground press' and uses modern technology such as the fax machine to create typographic images with enormous symbolic and visual potency.

Language, then, is an area of intense artistic speculation. The artists Cy Twombly, Anselm Kiefer, Jasper Johns and countless others struggle with the problems of establishing linguistic conventions in a multi-cultural, secular society. The graphic designer with an interest in letterforms would do well to explore the new areas that are opening up in the fine arts. Further technological developments such as interactive television, hypermedia and virtual reality will also continue to alter the way in which information may be given visible form.

As the work in this book has shown, the best graphic design communicates on many levels: literal, emotional and aesthetic. The quality of a design resides in its ability to address the viewer in an intelligent, articulate and exciting way. Hand lettering has a vital role to play in building a new approach to design. Talented lettering artists are coming onto the scene in increasing numbers. New

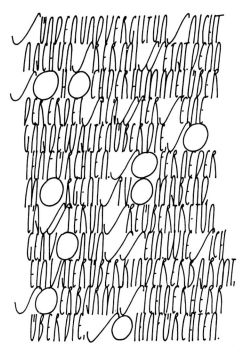

Experimental Calligraphy
A very different approach from Hans Schmidt's to the development of letterforms is evident in the word of the Berliner Hans-Joachim Burgert, whose emphasis is on the calligraphic line. According to him, calligraphy must strive to avoid the even textures and consistent geometry characteristic of most typefaces. Contrasts of shape, size, density and texture must be explored to the full. Burgert has developed his ideas by studying the principles underlying non-European calligraphic traditions.

LETTERING AND DESIGN
Hans-Joachim Burgert,
Berlin

145

Experimental Calligraphy
In Western culture, letters
have almost always shown
more function than form,
tending not to occupy the
central position in the fine
arts that they do in Arabic
and Asian cultures. The
work of Arthur Baker
attempts to rectify this,
joining artists such as Franz
Kline in his concentration
on the calligraphic mark.
But where Kline and other
abstract expressionists
denied the European
tradition of illusionism in
painting, Baker rejoices in
it. These calligraphic marks,
which were made in 1987
with large house-painting
brushes and ink on coated
paper, can hardly be
recognized as flat images.
The large composition to
the left appears to be a
sculpture of patinated
bronze. It is even provided
with an illusionistic base.

LETTERING Arthur Baker

technologies and new ways of using old technology are changing the way letters are made and applied. This book should help to advance the cause of hand-lettering by putting art directors and graphic designers in touch with the best lettering artists. It also shows the beauty, impact and heightened meaning that can grow out of a deeper understanding of the forms of letters. It is to be hoped that the challenge to use letters as tools of expressive and creative communication will be taken up by more and more designers and artists in the future.

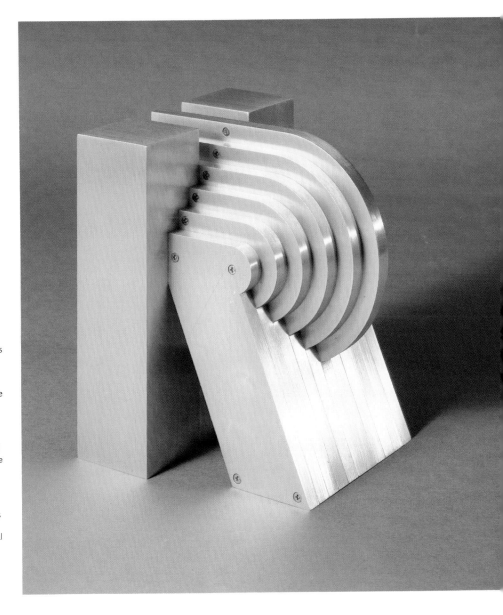

Sculpture
The twentieth century has seen the boundaries between the traditional artistic media dissolve. Thus Baker (opposite) gives a flat mark the appearance of sculpture, and here, Takenobu Igarashi gives actual sculptural form to the letter 'R'. There is a certain irony in this 1983 piece. The incredible precision with which the polished steel plates are engineered and bolted together lifts the sculpture out of the world of ordinary objects; the piece becomes pure form and is in a sense flattened. Igarashi, like Baker, crosses the boundaries between two- and three-dimensional form.

LETTERING AND DESIGN
Takenobu Igarashi, Tokyo
CLIENT Ricoh

Greetings Poster

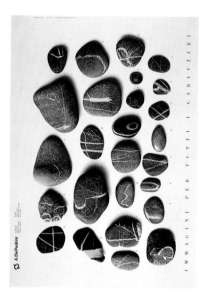

Found objects have played an important role in the work of many twentieth-century artists. They have been used to express the random and meaningless aspects of industrial culture, as well as the unpredictability of artistic inspiration. In this 1991 piece by Italo Lupi an alphabet is identified in the veins of river pebbles. Nature herself is seen here to be an artist, and the alphabet a divine creation. At the same time Italo Lupi is making a delightful pun: the Italian word for pebbles is 'pedrini'.

LETTERING AND DESIGN
Italo Lupi, Milan
CLIENT De Pedrini

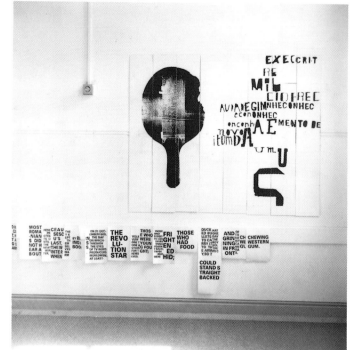

Fax Magazine

This conceptual piece was created by Simon Josebury and Paul Elliman in 1990 for Box Space, a magazine described by its creators as the 'overground press' - that is, a publication that combines the revolutionary energies of the underground press of the sixties with modern technology. This montage, which pairs fragments of political graffiti observed in Portugal with an enlarged ping-pong paddle found on the beach there, was one of several monumental images conceived for a faxed issue of the magazine. The revolutionary slogans observed by the artists in the streets of Lisbon seemed at odds with the languid atmosphere of the place. The ping-pong paddle can thus be read as an instrument of leisure or of violence.

LETTERING AND DESIGN
Simon Josebury and
Paul Elliman, London
CLIENT Box Space Magazine

Fax Magazine

This conceptual piece was created by Paul Elliman in 1991 for Box Space Magazine. Two flattened beer cans have been enlarged on the photocopier. The enlarged image was then cut into strips that were faxed to a small circle of friends who then reassembled the image in their studios. The generic processes of photocopying and faxing are thus humanized at the last stage, giving meaning to high-tech modes of communication. This piece also challenges expectations by changing the size of the image and by using the fax machine to create a monumental assembly. Paul Elliman and Peter Miles received gold and silver medals at the 1991 D&AD awards for their work on Box Space Magazine.

LETTERING AND DESIGN
Paul Elliman, London
CLIENT Box Space
Magazine, edited by Paul
Elliman and Peter Miles

New Directions

Alphabet of Bird Bones
The future of the alphabet is by no means secure. The digital revolution is causing designers to rethink the formal foundations of typefaces inherited from the age of lead and film. The concept of the global village challenges the supremacy of the Latin alphabet in the West. Joyce Cutler Shaw's experimental alphabet of bird bones (1988) is a response to our increasing awareness of other alphabetic traditions. Anatomically correct bird bones are used here to represent the twenty-six letters of the Latin alphabet. In order to identify the letters, we must observe details of form on a far more subtle level than is necessary with traditional letters.

LETTERING AND DESIGN
Joyce Cutler Shaw

Experimental Typeface
This poster, which accompanied the first issue of *Fuse*, features Ian Swift's experimental typeface Maze. Maze takes the process of reading out of the rational and into the intuitive realm. At first its stark geometric forms appear to be impenetrable, and may remind the viewer of modern Japanese typefaces. But the eyes will adjust themselves after a few moments and begin to recognize one letter, then another. In an instant the words become clear Through an intuitive leap the viewer learns to read all over again. Like all the fonts released through *Fuse*, Maze is an interactive digital font and its creators intend tht the user will further explore the limits of legibility.

DESIGN Ian Swift
CLIENT *Fuse*

Directory

The following directory lists more than one hundred designers from over twenty countries who are renowned for their innovative letterforms, whether hand-drawn or computer generated. Also given are associations of lettering artists where these exist, as well as graphic design and typography associations that can provide the names of lettering artists in particular countries. There are few organizations that bring together typographers, calligraphers, lettering artists, sign-writers and artists. Letter Exchange in the United Kingdom has pioneered a unified approach to the lettering arts, and it is to be hoped that similar organizations will be formed in other countries.

The question of when to bring in a professional lettering artist for a particular job is not easily answered. It is tempting for the designer to flip through an annual, find an appropriate style of lettering and apply it to a job. But to produce good lettering requires a sound understanding of letterforms, as well as a working knowledge of the tools and materials to be used. And since the detailed study of letterforms has not formed a part of the training of most graphic designers for several years, many would-be lettering artists lack the basic understanding required to produce forms of the highest quality. Weak forms can be disguised by texturing, layering and complex layout. Where the letters must stand on their own as pure form, it is best to seek professional assistance. It is all too common to see good designs compromised by bad lettering.

Designers who wish to further their studies of hand-lettering have a range of choices. Design and art colleges, though rarely offering extensive programmes in the design of letters, are normally willing to allow degree students to construct their own programmes of study in this area. Evening classes in typography may be able to teach basic principles, though computer courses that concentrate on letterforms are very rare indeed. Calligraphy courses abound, but are usually at a hobby level. The only exception to this for western calligraphy is the course taught at the Roehampton Institute in London, which is a full time programme for serious calligraphers. Annual conferences for typography and calligraphy take place in Europe and the USA. These provide excellent opportunities to study with leading practitioners and to meet others with the same interests.

Allen, Mark
Mark Allen and Associates
1601 Abbot Kinney Bvd
Venice, California 90291
U.S.A.

Tel. (310) 396 6471
Fax (310) 396 8697

Arab Consultants
9 rue de Clichy
75009 Paris
France

Tel. (01) 4526 8233
Fax (01) 4526 3932

von Arx-Anderson, Diane
3340 Bryant Avenue South
Minneapolis
Minnesota 55408
U.S.A.

Tel. (612) 825 6520

Åström, Magnus
Skolgatan 74
90246 Umeå
Sweden

Tel. (090) 129 495

Baines, Phil
10 Cornwall Gardens
Willesden Green
London NW10 2QX
Great Britain

Tel. (081) 451 3768

Baker, Arthur
Woods Road
Germantown, New York 12526
U.S.A.

Tel. (508) 687 0513

Barnbrook, Jonathan
Top Flat
90 Grays Inn Road
London WC1X 8AA
Great Britain

Tel. (071) 242 0966

Bernard, Pierre
Atelier de Creation
Graphique
7 rue de la Révolution
93100 Montreuil
France

Tel. (01) 4858 1353
Fax (01) 4870 9822

Bertram, Axel
Erich-Kurz-Strasse 9
1136 Berlin
Germany

Bigg, Chris
4AD
15-19 Alma Road
London SW18 1AA
Great Britain

Tel. (081) 870 9724
Fax (081) 874 6600

van Blokland, Erik
Laan van Meerdervoort IF
2517 AA Den Haag
Netherlands

Tel. (070) 360 5025
Fax (070) 310 6685

Boltana, François
45 rue René Sentanac
31300 Toulouse
France

Tel. (061) 49 30 48

Boudens, Pieter
Notenlarendreef 29
8200 Brugge
Belgium

Tel. (050) 38 47 91

Brody, Neville
Neville Brody Studios
65-69 East Road
London N1 6AH
Great Britain

Tel. (071) 253 5517
Fax (071) 253 5518

Burgermüllerbauer, Gestalter
Hauptstrasse 93
7507 Pfinztal 2
Germany

Tel. (07240) 1067
Fax (07240) 5103

Burgert, Hans-Joachim
Lassenstrasse 22
D - 1000 Berlin 33
Germany

Tel. (030) 826 4348

Büttner, Christine
BBC Television Centre
Wood Lane
London W12 7RJ

Tel. (081) 576 1680
Fax (081) 743 0377

Chase, Margo
Margo Chase Design
2255 Bancroft Avenue
Los Angeles,
California 90039
U.S.A.

Tel. (213) 668 1055
Fax (213) 668 2470

Checkland Kindleysides Design
Fowke Street
Rothley
Leicestershire LE7 7PJ
England

Tel. (0533) 3742 82
Fax (0533) 3746 49

Cicale, Annie
303 Barn Hill Road
Monroe
Connecticut 06468
U.S.A.

Tel. (203) 261 0470

Clough, James
Via Cezanne 11
20143 Milano
Italy

Tel. (02) 837 3915

Collett, Dickenson, Pearce and Partners Ltd
110 Euston Road
London NW1 2DQ
England

Tel. (071) 388 2424
Fax (071) 380 1217

The Creative Partnership
19 Greek Street
London W1V 5LF

Tel. (071) 439 7762
Fax (071) 437 1467
Offices also in
Los Angeles and Paris

Crescent Lodge Design Ltd
511/2 Barnsbury Street
London N1 1TP

Tel. (071) 607 6733
Fax (071) 609 6069

Culmone, Nancy
49 Pinnacle Road
Harvard
Massachusetts 01451
U.S.A.

Tel. (617) 456 6871

Currie, Leonard
50-54 Clerkenwell Road
London EC1M 5PS
Great Britain

Tel. (071) 251 3746
Fax (071) 253 7066

Deaver, Georgia
1045 Sansome Street
Suite 311
San Francisco
California 94111
U.S.A.

Tel. (415) 362 8960
Fax (415) 362 8577

Dieterich, Claude
4531 SW, 14th Street
Coral Gables
Florida 33134
U.S.A.

Dobkin, Joan
Cranbrook Academy of Art
500 Lone Pine Road
Box 801
Bloomfield Hills
Michigan 48303
U.S.A.

Tel. (313) 645 3336
Fax (313) 645 3327

Elliman, Paul
47 Lion Mills
392-396 Hackney Road
London E2 7AP
Great Britain

Tel. (071) 613 0378
Fax (071) 436 7165

English Markell Pockett
Bridle House
36 Bridle Lane
London W1R 3HJ
Great Britain

Tel. (071) 287 1155
Fax (071) 439 4203

Evans, Jean
142 Garden Street
Cambridge
Massachusetts 02138
U.S.A.

Tel. (617) 924 6050
Fax (617) 923 0857

Ezell, Reggie
2643 North Kimball
Chicago
Illinois 60647
U.S.A.

Tel. (312) 278 0677

Friedman, Liz
96 Selborne Road
Southgate
London N14 7DG
Great Britain

Tel. (081) 886 7484

Frutiger, Adrian
23 Ville Moderne
94110 Arcueil
France

Gallacher, Ethna
9 Jamieson Avenue
Fairlight
Sydney, N.S.W.
2094 Australia

Tel. (02) 949 4121
Fax (02) 949 4121

Garrett, Malcolm
Assorted Images
120 Curtain Road
London EC2
Great Britain

Tel. (071) 729 8044
Fax (071) 739 1973

Godson, Suzi
17 Fournier Street
Spitalfields
London E16 QE
Great Britain

Tel. (071) 377 6704
Fax (071) 377 6704

Greiman, April
April Greiman Inc
620 Moulton Avenue, No 211
Los Angeles
California 90031
U.S.A.

Tel.(213) 227 1222

Fax (213) 227 8651

Grundy, Peter
Grundy and Northedge
Thames Wharf Studios
Rainville Road
London W6 9HA
Great Britain

Tel. (071) 381 6217
Fax (071) 385 3344

Haanes, Christopher
Hesselberggatan 3
N 0555 Oslo
Norway

Tel. (02) 354123
Fax (02) 354123

Harris, David
Church House
Clyst St George
Devon EX3 ORE
Great Britain

Tel. (0392) 874 408

Harvey, Michael
4 Valley Road
Bridport
Dorset DT6 4JR
Great Britain

Tel. (0308) 227 77
Fax (0308) 421 548

Hoefer, Karlgeorg
Weilburgerweg 7
6050 Offenbach-am-Main
Germany

Homar, Lorenzo
Calle Estado 656
Miramar
Puerto Rico 00907

Horlbeck-Kappler, Irmgard
Dittrichring 14
7010 Leipzig
Germany

Hunger, Kirsten
Hochschule für Grafik
und Buchkunst Leipzig
Postfach 68
Dimitroffstrasse 11
0 - 7010 Leipzig
Germany

Tel. (041) 31 24 01
Fax (041) 41 91 32 11

Igarashi, Takenobu
Igarashi Studio
6-6-22 Minami-Aoyama
Minato-Ku, Tokyo
107 Japan

Tel. (03) 3498 3621
Fax (03) 3498 3669

Johnson, Iskra
1605 Twelfth Avenue
Suite 26
Seattle
Washington 98122
U.S.A.

Tel. (206) 323 8256
Fax (206) 323 6863

Kalman, Tibor
M & Co
50 West 17th Street
New York
NY 10011
U.S.A.

Tel. (212) 243 0082
Fax (212) 463 0523

Katsui, Mitsuo
Mitsuo Katsui Design Office
5-1-10-907 Minami-Aoyama
Minato-Ku
107 Tokyo
Japan

Tel. (03) 3407 0801
Fax (03) 3407 0845

Kindersley, Richard
40 Cardigan Street
London SE11 5PF
Great Britain

Tel. (071) 735 9374

Koeth, Alice
221 East 88th Street
New York
NY 10128
U.S.A.

Tel. (212) 831 4456

Koeweiden, Jacques
Koeweiden Postma Ontwerpers
W G Plein 516/AOC
1054 Amsterdam
Netherlands

Tel. (020) 612 1975
Fax (020) 616 9798

Kshirsagar, Santosh Bhaskar
6/13 Goregaonkar Lane
Girgaum
Bombay
400 004
India

Larcher, Jean
16 Chemin des Bourgognes
95000 Cergy-Pontoise
France

Tel. (01) 30 38 47 57

Lewandowski, T A
13 place Emile Goudeau
Atelier 4
Bâteau-Lavoir
75018 Paris
France

Lupi, Italo
39 via Vigevano
20144 Milan
Italy

Tel. (02) 89 40 39 50
Fax (02) 89 40 40 42

Lutz, Hans-Rudolf
Lessingstrasse 11
8002 Zürich
Switzerland

Tel. (01) 201 7672

Massachusetts Institute of Technology
Media Arts and Sciences,
Visible Language Workshop
20 Ames Street
Cambridge
Massachusetts 02139
U.S.A.

Tel. (617) 253 4416
Fax (617) 258 6264

Massee, Happy
605 Hudson Street, No 5N
New York
NY 10014
U.S.A.

Massoudy, Hassan
18 Quai de la Marne
75019 Paris
France

Matsunaga, Shin
Shin Matsunaga Design Inc
8th Floor
Ishibashi-Kogyo Building
7-3-1 Minami-Aoyama
Minato-Ku
Tokyo
107 Japan

Tel. (03) 3499 0291
Fax (03) 3499 3309

Morentz, Barry
320 East 23rd Street, No 4P
New York
New York 10010
U.S.A.

Tel. (212) 477 0198

Nagai, Kazumasa
Nippon Design Centre
Chuo-Daiwa Building
1-13-13 Ginza Chuo-Ku
Tokyo
Japan

Tel. (03) 3567 3231
Fax (03) 3535 3569

Nanbu, Toshiyasu
Taste Co Ltd
Ikkyu Building 5F
Shinkan 2-4-2 Tokiwa-Machi
Chuo-Ku
Osaka
Japan 540

Tel. (06) 947 5816
Fax (06) 947 5815

Neuenschwander, Brody
Spinolarei 2
8000 Bruges
Belgium

Tel. (050) 342 189
Fax (050) 345 529

Nyffeler, Roland
Gerenstrasse 25
CH 8305 Dietlikon
Switzerland

Tel. (01) 833 2982
Fax (01) 833 2982

Oatis, Mark
Smith, Nelson and Oatis
1441 46th Avenue, Unit 9
Denver
Colorado 80211
U.S.A.

Tel. (303) 433 5985
Fax (303) 477 8604

Ott, Nicolaus and Bernard Stein
Ott + Stein Gestaltung
Bundesplatz 17
1000 Berlin 31
Germany

Palav, Achyut
25 Rajkotwala Building
opp Ganesh Talkies
Lalbaug
Bombay 400 012
India

Tel. (022) 4140562

Pao, Derick
23 Becca Hall Trail
Scarborough
Ontario M1V 2T7
Canada

Tel. (416) 321 1907
Fax (416) 321 1908

Pentagram Design Ltd
11 Needham Road
London W11 2RP
Great Britain

Tel. (071) 229 3477
Fax (071) 727 9932

Perkins, Tom
40 High Street
Sutton
Ely
Cambridgeshire CB6 2RB
Great Britain

Tel. (0353) 778 328

Planungsteam
Lindenallee 9B
5000 Cologne 51
Germany

Tel. (0221) 38 89 29
Fax (0221) 38 56 65

Pott, Gottried
Im Weingarten 21A
Weisbaden 6200
Germany

Tel. (0611) 428360

Pronenko, Leonid
350065 Krasndar
Nevkipelova Street 15 67
Commonwealth of
Independent States

Quay, David
Studio 12
10-11 Archer Street
London W1V 7HG
Great Britain

Tel. (071) 734 6925
Fax (071) 734 2607

Raw, Stephen
1 Hartington Road
Chorlton-cum- Hardy
Manchester M21 8UZ
Great Britain

Tel. (061) 861 9241
Fax (061) 862 9497

Reichert, Josua
Pirschweg 39
D-8209 Haidholzen
Germany

Tel. (080 36) 593

Rohrs, Carl
228 Ocean View
Santa Cruz
California 95062
U.S.A.

Tel. (408) 429 8849

Ronchi, Anna
Via de Predis 2
20155 Milan
Italy

Tel. (02) 3932 3878
Fax (02) 3932 3878

van Rossum, Just
Bagijnastraat 4
2511 CK-Den Haag
Den Haag
Netherlands

Tel. (070) 362 5147

Rousselot, Ricardo
Rousselot, S A Design
Gran via Carlos III, 97-J 10B
Barcelona
08028 Spain

Tel. (093) 339 7850
Fax (093) 411 1216

Rowland, Ruth
Studio 5
Abbeville Mews
88 Clapham Park Road
London SW4 7BX
Great Britain

Tel. (071) 498 5319
Fax (071) 627 4714

Sack, Freda
Inglenook
Merle Common
Oxted
Surrey RH8 ORP
Great Britain

Tel. (0883) 722 131

Sato, Koichi
Koichi Sato Design Studio
1-35-28-504Hongo Bunkyo-Ku
Tokyo 113
Japan

Tel. (03) 3815 6630
Fax (03) 3815 6630

Schenk, Andreas
Reinsprung 2
CH-4051 Basel
Switzerland

Tel. (061) 261 3900

Schmidt, Hans
Schlossstrasse 8
5449 Baden Hard
Germany

Tel. (06746) 1353

Schneider, Werner
Am Langen Land 2
5928 Bad Laasphe
Germany

Tel. (02754) 453

Schumann, Heinz
Johannes-Schneider Strasse 13
9091 Karl-Marx-Stradt
Germany

Shaw, Joyce Cutler
7245 Rue de Roarc
La Jolla
California 92037
U.S.A.

Shaw, Paul
785 West End Avenue
New York
NY 10025
U.S.A.

Tel. (212) 666 3738
Fax (212) 666 2163

Skarsgard, Susan
807 Hutchins Street
Ann Arbor
Michigan 48103
U.S.A.

Tel. (313) 761 3192
Fax (313) 665 7487

Skogh, Cecilia
Skärmarbringksveien 21
Stockholm
Sweden

Tel. (08) 395 851

van Slingerland, Elmo
Burgemeester Baumannlaan 62C
3043 an Rotterdam/Overschie
Netherlands

Tel. (010) 262 3112

Spieker, Ewald
Groenburgwal 63
1011 ht Amsterdam
Netherlands

Tel. (020) 623 8552

Stylorouge
18A-20 Brook Mews North
London W2

Tel. (071) 723 3511
Fax (071) 262 2598

Tanahashi, Kazuaki
1520 Blake Street
Berkeley
California 94703
U.S.A.

Tel. (415) 649 8844

Thompson, Philip
35 Elgin Crescent
London W11 2JD
Great Britain

Tel. (071) 221 1925

Veljovic, Jovica
Oldenfeldstieg 3A
22143 Hamburg
Germany

Tel. (040) 679 1910

**J Walter Thompson
Co., Ltd.**
40 Berkeley Square
London W1X 6AD
Great Britain

Tel. (071) 499 4040
Fax (071) 493 8432

Waters, Julian
23707 Woodfield Road
Gaithersburg
Maryland 20882
U.S.A.

Tel. (301) 253 3422
Fax (301) 972 2271

Why Not Associates
10-11 Archer Street
London W1V 7HG
Great Britain

Tel. (071) 494 0762
Fax (071) 494 0678

Yelland, Jill
18E/19 Parker Street
South Perth 615
Western Australia

Tel. (09) 367 6679

INTERNATIONAL

ICOGRADA
International Council of
Graphic Design
Associations
PO Box 398
London W11 4UG

Tel. (071) 603 8494
Fax (071) 371 6040

AUSTRALIA

**Graphic Arts Services
Association of
Australia**
32 Buckingham Street
Surrey Hills
NSW 2010

Tel. (612) 319 3311

**Crafts Council of
Australia**
35 George Street
Sydney
NSW 2000

Tel. (02) 241 1701
Fax (02) 247 6143

BELGIUM

Scriptores
Secretary: Marion Stoffels
Kloosterstraat 183
2000 Antwerpen

Tel. (03) 216 9484

CANADA

**Canadian Crafts
Council**
189 Laurier Avenue East
Ottawa
Ontario K1N 6PL

Tel. (613) 235 8200
Fax (613) 235 7425

**The Society of Graphic
Designers of Canada**
Ontario Chapter
260 King Street East
Toronto
Ontario M5A 1K3
Canada

**Montreal Calligraphy
Society**
c/o Ms Marion Zimmer
687 Grosvenor Avenue
Westmount
Quebec H3Y 2T1

**Ottawa Calligraphy
Society**
c/o Ms Linda Cloutier
181 Huntridge-Priv
Ottawa
Ontario K1V 9J3

**Calligraphic Arts Guild
of Toronto**
PO Box 115 Willowdale
Station A
North York
Ontario M2N 5S7

DENMARK

**Grafiske
Organisationer**
Landemarket 11
PO Box 2210
1018 Copenhagen

Tel. (033) 156040

FRANCE

**Association des
Agences Conseils en
Communication**
40 Boulevard Malesherbes
75008 Paris

Tel. (01) 47 42 13 42

**Association
Internationale du
Nouvel Objet Visuel**
Catherine Brelet
27 Rue de l'Université
Paris

Tel. (01) 42 61 58 54

Graphiés
Le Vieux Logis de l'Alberge
44470 Mauves-sur-Loire

Tel. (01) 40 25 54 16

**Société
d'Encouragement aux
Métiers d'Art**
20 Rue de la Boétie
75008 Paris

Tel. (01) 42 65 74 50

**Syndicat National des
Graphistes**
25 Rue de la Bienfaisance
75008 Paris

Tel. (01) 42 93 61 07

GERMANY

ATypl
Secretariat: c/o NTC Nordic
Trade Center
Eggerstadstrasse 13
D-2300 Kiel 1

Tel. (0431) 97406
Fax (0431) 9740630

**Bund Deutscher Grafik-
Designer E.V.**
Altestadt 8
4000 Düsseldorf 1

Tel. (0211) 80448
Fax (0211) 134109

**Bundesverband
Kunsthandwerk E.V.**
Bleichstrasse 38a
D-6000 Frankfurt 1

Tel. (069) 280510
Fax (069) 20097

Klingspor Museum
(Museum of the Graphic
Arts)
6050 Offenbach-am-Main

Tel. (069) 8065 2954
Fax (069) 800 2192

**Schreibwerkstatt
Klingspor Offenbach**
Förderkreis für
Internationaler Kalligraphie
(Society for the Promotion
of International Calligraphy)
Weilburgerweg 7
6050 Offenbach-am-Main

Tel. (069) 862 069

GREAT BRITAIN

**The Chartered Society
of Designers**
29 Bedford Square
London WC1

Tel. (071) 631 1510
Fax (071) 580 2338

**Crafts Council of
England and Wales**
44A Pentonville Road
London N1 9BY

Tel. (071) 278 7700
Fax (071) 837 6891

**Design Business
Association**
29 Bedford Square
London WC1

Tel. (071) 631 1510
Fax (071) 580 2338

Design Council
28 Haymarket
London SW1

Tel. (071) 839 8000
Fax (071) 925 2130

Letter Exchange
Secretary: Sue Cavendish
54 Boileau Road
London SW13 9BL

Tel. (081) 748 9951

**Society of Typographic
Designers**
Attention: John Harrison
21--27 Seagrave Road
London SW6 1RP

Tel. (071) 381 4258
Fax (071) 385 8726

**Society of Scribes and
Illuminators**
Secretary: Sue Cavendish
54 Boileau Road
London SW13 9BL

Tel. (081) 748 9951

ITALY

**Associazione
Calligrafica Italiana**
Secretary: Anna Ronchi
Via de Predis 2
20155 Milan

Tel. (02) 39 32 38 78
Fax (02) 39 32 38 78

Assografici
Piazza Conciliazione, 1
20123 Milan

Tel. (02) 49 81 051
Fax (02) 48 16 947

JAPAN

**Japan Graphic Design
Association**
2-11-14 Minami-Aoyama
Minato-Ku
Tokyo 107

Tel. (03) 3404 2557
Fax (03) 3404 2554

**Japan Typography
Association**
CC Centre
4-8-15 Yushima
Bunkyo-Ku
Tokyo 113

Fax (03) 3812 7268

THE NETHERLANDS

Dutch Form
Waterlooplein 211
1011 PG Amsterdam

Tel. (020) 38 11 20

**Beroepsvereniging
Nederlandse
Ontwerpers**
(Dutch Society of
Designers)
Waterlooplein 219
1011 PG Amsterdam

Tel. (020) 6244748
Fax (020) 627 8585

Scriptores
Secretary: Anneke Linssen
Heidestraat 5
6114-AA Susteren

Tel: (04499) 397

NORWAY

Grafisk Institutt
Gaustadalleen 21
0371 Oslo

Tel. (02) 95 85 50
Fax (02) 60 28 18

POLAND

**Polskich Artystow
Grafikow Projektantow**
Nowy Swiat 7
00496 Warsaw

Tel. (022) 215143

SPAIN

AA-FAD
(Crafts Council
of Spain)
Brusi 45
08006 Barcelona

Tel. (03) 209 11 55

**Asociación de
Diseñadores Graficos**
Brusi 45
08006 Barcelona

Tel. (03) 209 1155

SWEDEN

**Grafiska
Industriföreningen**
Blasieholmsgatan 4A
11148 Stockholm

Tel. (08) 762 6800
Fax (08) 611 0828

SWITZERLAND

**Arbeitsgemeinschaft
Schweizer Grafiker**
Limmatstrasse 63
8005 Zürich

Tel. (01) 272 4555
Fax (01) 272 5282

Crafts Council Schweiz
Case Postale 898
2501 Biel-Beinne

Tel. (032) 51 63 69

**Schweizerische
Kalligraphische
Gesellschaft**
Gerenstrasse 25
8305 Dietlikon

Tel. (01) 933 2982
Fax (01) 933 2982

USA

**American Institute of
Graphic Art**
1059 3rd Avenue
New York
NY 10021

Tel. (212) 752 0813
Fax (212) 755 6749

American Craft Council
72 Spring Street
New York
NY 10012

Tel. (212) 274 0630
Fax (212) 274 0650

**The Friends of
Calligraphy**
PO Box 5194
San Francisco
California 94101

**International Letter
Arts Network**
PO Box 26229
Santa Ana
California 92799

Tel. (714) 541 4171
Fax (714) 893 0082

Society of Scribes
PO Box 933
New York
NY 10150

Type Directors Club
60 East 42nd Street,
Suite 1416
New York,
NY 10165

Tel. (212) 983 6042
Fax (212) 983 6043

Letterform and Spacing

BENSON, JOHN HOWARD and ARTHUR GRAHAM CAREY. *The Elements of Lettering.* McGraw-Hill Book Company, New York 1950

CATICH, EDWARD M. *The Origin of the Serif: Brush Writing and Roman Letters.* 2nd ed. Catich Gallery, St Ambrose University, Davenport, Iowa 1991

DOWDING, G. *Finer Points in the Spacing and Arrangement of Type.* Wace and Company, London 1954

GOUDY, FREDERICK W. *The Capitals from the Trajan Column.* Oxford University Press, Oxford and New York 1936

KAECH, WALTER. *Rhythm and Proportion in Lettering.* Walter-Verlag 1956

Legibility

CROWDER, R. *The Psychology of Reading.* Oxford University Press, New York and Oxford 1982

REYNOLDS, LINDA. Legibility of Type, *Baseline International Typographics Journal.* (Cassandre issue) 1988, pp. 26-29

SPENCER, HERBERT. *The Visible Word.* Lund Humphries, London 1969

SWANN, CAL. *Language and Typography.* Lund Humphries, London 1991

Calligraphy

CAMP, ANN. *Pen Lettering.* A & C Black, London (USA: Taplinger) 1984

CHILD, HEATHER, ed. *The Calligrapher's Handbook.* A & C Black, London 1986

FAIRBANK, ALFRED. *A Handwriting Manual,* Dryad Press, Leicester 1932

HARVEY, MICHAEL. *Calligraphy in the Graphic Arts.* The Bodley Head, London 1988

JOHNSTON, EDWARD. *Writing and Illuminating, and Lettering.* 32nd ed., Pitman Publishing Ltd, London 1975. Now published by A & C Black, London

PEARCE, CHARLES. *The Little Manual of Calligraphy.* William Collins Sons and Co Ltd, London 1982

Drawn Letters

GRAY, NICOLETE. *Lettering as Drawing.* Oxford Paperbacks, Oxford 1970

HARVEY, MICHAEL. *Creative Lettering: Drawing and Design.* The Bodley Head, London 1985

HARVEY, MICHAEL. *Lettering Design.* The Bodley Head, London 1975

Further Reading

Architectural Lettering

BARTRAM, ALAN. *Lettering in Architecture.* Lund Humphries, London 1975

GRAY, NICOLETE. *Lettering on Buildings.* Architectural Press, London 1960

KINDERSLEY, DAVID and LIDA LOPES CARDOZO. *Letters Slate Cut.* Lund Humphries (USA: Taplinger) 1981

Digital Design

BIGELOW, CHUCK and DONALD DAY, Digital Typography, *Scientific American.* August 1983, pp. 106-119

GREIMAN, APRIL. *Hybrid Imagery,* Architecture Design & Technology Press, London 1990

HEWSON, DAVID. *Introduction to Desktop Publishing.* Fraser, London 1988

KAROW, PETER. *Digital Formats for Typefaces.* URW, Hamburg 1988

STONE, SUMNER. *Typography on the Personal Computer.* Lund Humphries, London 1991. (USA ed. *On Stone: Typography on the Personal Computer.* Bedford Arts, San Francisco 1991)

Typography

BAUDIN, FERNAND. *How Typography Works (And Why it is Important).* Lund Humphries, London 1991

BOOTH-CLIBBORN, EDWARD and RICK POYNOR, eds. *New Wave Typography.* Internos Books/Booth-Clibborn Editions, London 1991

CARTER, ROB, BEN DAY and PHILIP MEGGS. *Typographic Design: Form and Communication.* Van Nostrand Reinhold, New York 1985

GORDON, MAGGIE and EUGENIE DODD. *Decorative Typography.* Phaidon Press Ltd, Oxford 1990

LUTZ, HANS RUDOLF. *Ausbildung in Typografischer Gestaltung.* 2nd ed., Karlheinz Biersack GmbH, Constance 1989

MCLEAN, RUARI, *The Thames and Hudson Manual of Typography.* Thames and Hudson, London 1988.

SPENCER, HERBERT. *Pioneers of Modern Typography.* 2nd ed., Lund Humphries, London 1982

TRACY, WALTER. *Letters of Credit: A View of Type Design.* Gordon Fraser, London 1986

ZAPF, HERMANN. *Hermann Zapf and his Design Philosophy.* Society of Typographic Arts, Chicago 1987